CANADA'S
CULINARY HERITAGE

100 RECIPES FROM NOTABLE CANADIANS

Klorofil
ÉDITIONS | PUBLISHING

COORDINATOR: Sylvain Perron

PROJECT MANAGERS: Rachel Beechey, Catherine Boulay, Annik Boivin, Nathalie Ayotte and Julie Bordeleau

CHEFS: Caroline Poirier, Michel Daigle and Nicolas Tremblay

PHOTOGRAPHY & PHOTO EDITING: Karyne Gagné

ACCESSORIES: Stokes and Aubépine collections de céramiques

WRITING AND TRANSLATION: Natasha Leroux and Noemi LoPinto

PROOFREADING: Nicole Beechey and Marie Martel

COVER DESIGN: Marianne Parent and Josée Bouchard

LAYOUT: Josée Bouchard

SPECIAL COLLABORATION: Chicoutimi Golf Club

PHOTO CREDITS: Philippe Renault / picturescanada.com (pages 8, 10, 12), Raffi Tutundijan (page 170), Guylain Doyle (page 186)

PUBLISHER: Klorofil Publishing

ISBN: 978-2-9810783-7-7

LEGAL DEPOSIT – Bibliothèque et Archives nationales du Québec, 2017
LEGAL DEPOSIT – Library and Archives Canada, 2017

Digital format available.
Bulk sales available.

If you are promoting activities to improve well-being at the workplace, celebrating a special anniversary or planning a fundraising event, Klorofil can help you put together a cookbook showcasing your employees or members of your family or your community.

CONTENTS

Sylvain Perron
Publisher

A WORD FROM THE PUBLISHER

As part of the celebrations surrounding Canada's 150th anniversary, it is with great pleasure that Klorofil Publishing presents a cookbook for Canadians by Canadians. This cookbook will reunite residents from across the country and presents a journey from coast to coast through pages of mouth-watering recipes from our diverse cultural population.

The individuals, who unveil their favorite recipe, do so out of generosity and their contribution is greatly appreciated. These recreational chefs graciously share a glimpse into their childhood memories and family heritage.

As a collector's item, besides paying tribute to the culinary art of cooking, you will learn about products from your local area and discover new products from across the country.

I know that my fellow Canadians will find great joy in preparing these recipes from the individuals who represent our country while at home or travelling abroad. You can also take pride in knowing that you're helping to contribute to Breakfast Club of Canada's financial health through this appetizing project.

Have fun sharing!

Sylvain Perron
Publisher
Klorofil inc.

The Honourable Mélanie Joly
Canadian Heritage

A WORD FROM CANADIAN HERITAGE

As Minister of Canadian Heritage, I commend everyone who dedicated their time and effort to making this amazing book of recipes possible.

Diversity is one of Canada's greatest strengths. Our country was built by men and women who represent all faiths and cultures and speak a multitude of languages. What a wonderful idea it is to publish a cookbook that reflects this rich diversity in honour of the 150th anniversary of Confederation!

Happy reading! I wish you many delicious discoveries.

The Honourable Mélanie Joly
Canadian Heritage

Daniel Germain
Breakfast Club of Canada

A WORD FROM BREAKFAST CLUB OF CANADA

When I founded Breakfast Club in 1994, my mission was to help children have an equal chance of academic success by providing a good full and nutritious breakfast in a warm and nurturing environment. Today, thanks to our volunteers and partners, over 163,000 children are fed daily throughout Canada.

But the Club is about more than just breakfast. It is also a social project.

In this recipe book, you'll find a new source of inspiration for your menus and I hope it will inspire many family gatherings.

On behalf of all the children of the Club, I wish you "bon appétit" and above all, THANK YOU for helping them grow… one breakfast at a time!

Daniel Germain
President and Founder, Breakfast Club of Canada

THANK YOU TO OUR CONTRIBUTORS

Manjit Minhas

Marina Orsini

Kathleen Wynne

Bernard Derome

Robert Munsch

Véronic DiCaire

Annie Dufresne

Claudia Bunce

Keshia Chanté

Geneviève Borne

Martin Cauchon

Rick Hansen

Brian Pallister

Kevin Parent

Alain Vigneault

Alexandre Tagliani

Lise Watier

Melinda Rogers

Arthur B. McDonald

Joé Juneau

Terri Clark

Roger Mooking

Dawna Friesen

Caroline Ouellette

Jean-Philippe Wauthier

Lisa LaFlamme

Martine Mai

Bret Hart

Angela Liddon

Sandy Silver

Mary Walsh

Louis-François Marcotte

Michael Smith

Hayley Wickenheiser

Mike Weir

Mike Holmes

Bruny Surin

Serena Ryder

Scotty Bowman

Martin Picard

Ron James

Elizabeth Manley

Nancy Greene

Alex Harvey

Jonas Tomalty

Monique F. Leroux

Marianne St-Gelais

Chantal Petitclerc

Penny Oleksiak

Alain Bouchard

Michaëlle Jean

Lysanne Richard

Carey Price

Alex Trebek

Roméo Dallaire

Catriona Le May Doan

Sean Power

Bryan Baeumler

Stephen McNeil

Oliver Jones

Brian Orser

Aaron Pritchett

Lynn Crawford

Nicole Jones

Tyler Shaw

Valérie Maltais

Yves Desjardins-Siciliano

Rachel Notley

Rich Little

Marie-Christine Depestre

Sophie Lui

Jeanne Beker

Colm Feore

Susur Lee

Brad Wall

Mikaël Kingsbury

Charles & François Hamelin

Caitlin Cronenberg

Peter Miller

Rodger Brulotte

Brian Gallant

Philippe Couillard

Christy Clark

k.d. lang

David Walmsley

Clara Hughes

Pierre Lavoie

Daniel Lanois

Joannie Rochette

Rick Campanelli

George Canyon

Wayne Gretzky

Darrin Rose

Ingrid Falaise

Sean Cheesman

Guy Lafleur

Jennifer Jones

Bonnie Brooks

Paul Martin

David St-Jacques

Wade MacLauchlan

CANADIAN TULIP FESTIVAL – OTTAWA, ON

THIS & THAT

"This recipe is by my mother, Rani."

ALOO GOBI
(POTATO AND CAULIFLOWER CURRY)

Manjit Minhas
Calgary, AB

Co-founder and CEO of Minhas Breweries & Distilleries and
Dragon on Dragons' Den

SERVINGS 8–10 / PREPARATION 20 MIN / COOKING 25 MIN

INGREDIENTS

60 ml (4 tbsp)	oil
1	large onion, chopped
5 ml (1 tsp)	cumin seeds
1 bunch	fresh cilantro, stalks and leaves, chopped separately
10 ml (2 tsp)	turmeric
5 ml (1 tsp)	salt
1	small green chili pepper, minced or 5 ml (1 tsp) chili powder
125 ml (½ cup)	diced tomatoes (canned)
2.5 cm (1 in)	fresh ginger, peeled, grated
2	cloves of garlic, minced
2	large potatoes, peeled, cut into even pieces
1	large cauliflower, leaves removed, cut evenly into eighths
10 ml (2 tsp)	ground garam masala

PREPARATION

1. Heat vegetable oil in a large saucepan over medium heat.
2. Add the onion and cumin seeds to the oil.
3. Stir together and cook until onions become creamy and translucent.
4. Add chopped cilantro stalks, turmeric, salt and chili, to taste.
5. Add tomatoes, ginger and garlic; mix thoroughly.
6. Add potatoes and cauliflower to the sauce plus a few tablespoons of water to ensure that the mixture doesn't stick to the saucepan.
7. Ensure that the potatoes and cauliflower are coated with the curry sauce.
8. Cover and allow to simmer for 20 minutes or until potatoes are cooked.
9. Add garam masala and stir.
10. Sprinkle chopped cilantro leaves on top of the curry.
11. Turn off the heat, cover, and leave for as long as possible before serving.

"I love hiking in Banff in the summer and skiing in Banff with my husband and my two young girls."

"I created this recipe because I was always looking for quick new interesting smoothie recipes as I drink so many of them. I chose this one because it's the same one I submitted to a cookbook that honours my dear friend Grace Bowen, who passed away at 10 years old from childhood cancer."

AVOCADO SLIPPERY SMOOTH SHAKE

Hayley Wickenheiser
Shaunavon, SK

Olympic Medallist in Women's Hockey

SERVING 1 / PREPARATION 5 MIN

INGREDIENTS

1	ripe avocado
375—500 ml (1 ½–2 cups)	almond milk original (no flavour)
1 scoop	vanilla whey protein powder (optional)
250 ml (1 cup)	frozen blueberries
½	banana (optional)
3 ml (½ tsp)	cinnamon
	Ice (optional)

PREPARATION

1. Put all ingredients together in a blender. Blend for desired smoothness.

" *Enjoy!* **"**

" *I like to use Precision Grass Fed Whey Protein.* **"**

 "About Canada, I love pretty much everything! It's the greatest. I love to play outdoors in the mountains, bike our beautiful trail system, eat at our amazing restaurants and more."

21

"Before I became vegetarian, gluten free, fair trade and organic… (eye roll), as a kid I ate something that I later began to refer to as Canadian S'mores. They are a fond memory of my childhood… a simple but most delicious treat. It is one of my best childhood memories and worth a try for sure."

CANADIAN S'MORE

k.d. lang
Calgary, AB

Singer and Musician

SERVINGS 12 / PREPARATION 10 MIN / COOKING 13–15 MIN

INGREDIENTS

Ritz crackers
Butter
Cheez Whiz
Marshmallows

PREPARATION

Preheat oven to 230°C (450°F)

1. Place 12 Ritz crackers on a baking tray (you could use the organic Late July brand or some other variation).
2. Put a dollop of butter, Cheez Whiz (which is my Canadian favourite and definitely not available in an organic form since it is spelled with a Z), and put a marshmallow (vegetarian marshmallows actually exist!) on top of each cracker.
3. Bake until the marshmallows melt… and you have Canadian s'mores!

" *Variations: cheese flavoured Ritz crackers, Nutella, you name it.* "

 "I love walking by the rivers."

"This one is for all carrot cake fans! Creamy, crunchy, chewy and sweet, this recipe bursts with warming spices, a delightful (and oh-so-Canadian!) touch of pure maple syrup, and a full cup of carrots. This oatmeal is also wonderful as part of a holiday breakfast with loved ones (the serving size can be scaled up). I love serving it with coconut whipped cream to take it over the top!"

CARROT CAKE OATMEAL

Angela Liddon
Oakville, ON

Founder, Oh She Glows

SERVINGS 2–3 / PREPARATION 15 MIN / COOKING 10 MIN

INGREDIENTS

Oatmeal

250 ml (1 cup)	finely grated peeled carrot
310 ml (1 ¼ cups)	unsweetened almond milk (more as needed)
20 ml (1 tbsp + 1 tsp)	pure maple syrup
5 ml (1 tsp)	ground cinnamon
1.25 ml (¼ tsp)	ground ginger
1 dash	ground nutmeg, to taste
1 pinch	fine sea salt
125 ml (½ cup)	gluten-free rolled oats
5 ml (1 tsp)	pure vanilla extract
1.25—2.5 ml (¼–½ tsp)	fresh lemon juice (optional)

Topping Suggestions

Chopped toasted walnuts

Coconut whipped cream

Pure maple syrup

Raisins

Shredded coconut

Cinnamon

PREPARATION

1. Peel and finely grate the carrots on a box grater. Use the finest grate, rather than the standard size, so the carrot shreds are very small. This helps the carrot cook quickly and blend into the oats.
2. In a medium-sized pot over medium heat, whisk together the almond milk, maple syrup, cinnamon, ginger, nutmeg and a pinch of salt until smooth.
3. Stir in the grated carrots and oats.
4. Bring to a low boil and then reduce the heat to medium and let simmer. Cook, uncovered, for about 10 minutes, stirring frequently until thickened. If it is too thick, stir in another 15 ml (1 tbsp) of almond milk.
5. Remove from heat and stir in the vanilla extract. If desired, stir in a bit of lemon juice to make the flavours pop.
6. Portion into bowls and garnish with your desired toppings.
7. Enjoy immediately.

" *Leftovers can be stored in an airtight container in the fridge for a couple days. They are also delicious cold!* "

"I've only had the opportunity to visit a few times, but Banff has some of the most stunning views I've ever seen and I can't wait to go back. Hiking along the Emerald Lake trail, the water is turquoise and there are mountains everywhere you look. So spectacular!"

"I make these muffins for my 3-year-old son, Elliot, who loves them! Mom likes them as well because in addition to the dark chocolate, there is lots of fibre! This is a recipe by Ricardo that I modified slightly by reducing the amount of chocolate and it's just as good!"

CHOCOLICIOUS MUFFINS

The Honourable Chantal Petitclerc
Grandville, QC

Credit: Martin Girard

Senator and Paralympic Medallist in Wheelchair Racing

SERVINGS 12 / PREPARATION 10 MIN / COOKING 20 MIN

INGREDIENTS

375 ml (1 ½ cups)	wheat bran cereal, such as All-Bran
250 ml (1 cup)	milk
2.5 ml (½ tsp)	vanilla extract
250 ml (1 cup)	unbleached all-purpose flour
60 ml (¼ cup)	cocoa
5 ml (1 tsp)	baking powder
5 ml (1 tsp)	baking soda
1.25 ml (¼ tsp)	salt
1	egg
125 ml (½ cup)	brown sugar, lightly packed
60 ml (¼ cup)	canola oil
190 ml (¾ cup)	dark chocolate, chopped

PREPARATION

Preheat oven to 180°C (350°F)—with rack in the middle position

1. Line a muffin tin with paper or silicone liners.
2. In a bowl, combine the cereal, milk and vanilla; set aside.
3. In another bowl, combine the flour, cocoa, baking powder, baking soda and salt; set aside.
4. In a third bowl, whisk together the egg, brown sugar and oil.
5. Add the cereal mixture and the dried ingredients to the third bowl. Using a spatula, mix until the dry ingredients are slightly moistened. Keep a few chocolate pieces to garnish the muffins and add the rest to the batter.
6. Spoon the batter into the muffin cups, up to the rim; garnish with chocolate.
7. Bake for about 20 minutes, or until a toothpick inserted into the centre of a muffin comes out clean; then remove and let cool.

♡ *"I love the Parc National du Bic. I can't get enough of this area. I did kayaking there a few years ago, it is magnificent and in addition to nature, there are beautiful lodges, gourmet bakeries and exceptional restaurants. It is definitely a place to discover."*

"This is my spouse's Elsa's recipe that we like to share with our friends in Lac Sept-Îles, Quebec."

Joé Juneau
Pont-Rouge, QC

Former NHL Hockey Player and Consultant

ELSA'S SALSA

SERVINGS 4 / PREPARATION 15 MIN

INGREDIENTS

4	fresh tomatoes, seeded
1	corn (ideally from Neuville, it's the best!)
	Red onion, chopped, to taste
	Cilantro (I usually put a lot)
1	clove of garlic, minced
1	red or yellow bell pepper, chopped
½–1	lime, juiced
	Oil
	Salt
	Sambal Oelek or hot pepper, to taste

To Serve

Tortillas, sour cream and guacamole

PREPARATION

1. Cut and dice the tomatoes in small enough pieces to fit in a tortilla chip.
2. Wrap the corn in a paper towel and cook in the microwave 2 minutes. Let cool and cut.
3. Juice the half or whole lime. Add lime juice and all other ingredients to a large bowl and mix well. Season, to taste.
4. Serve with sour cream, guacamole (avocado, oil, crushed garlic) and tortilla chips.

" *For a complete meal, add mango and shrimps. Accompany with a lager, white beer or a margarita.* "

"I appreciate Hockey School Development Programs, particularly the one for youth in Nunavik."

"This is my gracious wife's recipe."

FARMER'S BREAKFAST SKILLET

Bryan Baeumler
Burlington, ON

Host and TV Personality on HGTV Canada

SERVINGS 4–6 / PREPARATION 10 MIN / COOKING 30 MIN

INGREDIENTS

4–6	medium potatoes, cubed
45 ml (3 tbsp)	butter
1	small onion, finely chopped
1	garlic clove, minced
½	green or red bell pepper, finely chopped
250 ml (1 cup)	ham, diced
225 g (½ lb)	bacon, cooked, crumbled
	Salt and pepper
1 pinch	ground thyme

PREPARATION

Preheat the oven to 120°C (250°F)

1. Boil your potatoes in a large pot of water 5–7 minutes. They should be firm and not quite done. Drain and rinse in cold water; set aside.
2. Melt butter in a large skillet over medium heat. Add onion and garlic, and sauté until softened, about 4 minutes.
3. Add the bell pepper and sauté another 2 minutes.
4. Add the remaining ingredients, including potatoes, and mix well.
5. Cook hash until well browned, at least 10 minutes, stirring occasionally. In order to firm it up a little more, place in a medium baking dish and pop it in the oven while cooking the rest of the meal; serve warm.
6. Top with grated cheese and fried eggs, if desired.

"I love fishing in northern British Columbia!"

*"This bannock recipe is the one I use at home.
When we were hunting and camping in the Itcha Ilgachuz mountain range,
I substituted water for the milk and eggs. This recipe belongs to my grandmother, Theresa Holte."*

GRAN'S BANNOCK HOME RECIPE

Carey Price
Anahim Lake, BC

NHL Hockey Player

SERVINGS 6–8 / PREPARATION 5 MIN / COOKING 10 MIN

INGREDIENTS

680 ml (2 ¾ cups)	white flour
10 ml (2 tsp)	baking powder
5 ml (1 tsp)	salt
30 ml (2 tbsp)	shortening
375 ml (1 ½ cups)	warm milk
1	egg

PREPARATION

1. Sift together the flour, baking powder and salt.
2. Add the shortening and use a pastry cutter to cut it into fine crumbs.
3. In a separate bowl, beat together the milk and egg.
4. Create a well in the dry ingredients and add the liquid mixture. Mix well and form a nice ball. Knead the dough for no more than ten seconds to keep the dough soft. Add flour if necessary.
5. Create 6–8 oval shaped pieces of bannock about the size of a small hand.
6. Cook on medium-high temperature in a frying pan coated with oil. Make sure you have enough oil on the bottom of the pan and cook in a well-ventilated area.
7. The bannock will brown in approximately 8 minutes. Then turn the bannock over to cook the other side for approximately 8 minutes longer.
8. Serve warm; it is also good at room temperature.

" *You can also be creative and separate your dough into three separate bowls and add the following ingredients separately for variation: grated cheese, blueberries or raisins.* "

"I love hunting and camping in the Itcha Ilgachuz mountain range."

"The origins is that recipe are lost in the mists of time."

HOT SMOKIES

Mary Walsh
St John's, NL

Actress and Comedian

SERVINGS 2–3 / PREPARATION 5 MIN / COOKING 10–15 MIN

INGREDIENTS

1	large fillet of smoked cod
2	large tomatoes, diced
375 ml (1 ½ cups)	whipping cream
1 pinch	nutmeg (optional)

PREPARATION

1. Place the cod and tomatoes in a heavy-bottomed saucepan with the whipping cream.
2. Heat gently 10–15 minutes.
3. Serve in a small bowl or cup with some great French bread.

" *Totally simple and totally delicious.* "

"My favourite thing to do in Canada is visit Gros Morne National Park."

"When I was a child my father made porridge every morning before he went to work.
He used a double boiler and left it on low, but by the time us kids had it for breakfast
it was all congealed and yucky. This is very different! Enjoy!"

MY FAMOUS HOT & EASY BREAKFAST

**The Honourable
Nancy Greene Raine**
Sun Peaks, BC

Credit: Sam Egan

Senator, Olympic Medallist in Downhill Skiing

SERVINGS 2 / PREPARATION 15 MIN

INGREDIENTS

170—250 ml (⅔–1 cup)	water
10	unsalted raw almonds, approximately
½	apple chopped with skin on
75—180 ml (⅓–¾ cup)	good quality muesli (with dried raisins or dried cranberries)

Garnish

Milk, plain full-fat Greek yogurt, homemade jam or maple syrup

PREPARATION

1. Add water to a small pot with a tight-fitting lid. Put the pot on the stove and turn the element to high. Add a small handful of unsalted raw almonds.
2. Stir in apple and muesli. Add enough of the muesli until there is just a bit of liquid showing. Bring to a boil.
3. Put on the tight-fitting lid and turn off the heat.
4. Serve the hot cereal with milk and plain full-fat Greek yogurt with some homemade jam or maple syrup to sweeten it a bit.

   Note: If you have a ceramic stove top, move the pot to the warming element, turned on low. If you leave it on the element, it will cook too much on the bottom even though you've turned it off.

   Go and have your shower and when you come back the cereal will be nicely cooked.

" *You can see this is a 'Just Do It' type of recipe. It won't take long to figure out how you like it. It's quick and easy, and has a nice loose texture. If you buy ingredients in bulk and make your own muesli mix, it can be pretty inexpensive. It's nutritious and keeps you going all morning, even on the ski slopes.* "

 "I love Canada's amazing geography. I've travelled all over Canada, to every province and territory, and no matter where you go you can find beautiful natural places. We are so blessed to live in such a big country."

"One of my creation!"

PENNY'S EGGS & GUAC ON TOAST WITH A STRAWBERRY BANANA SMOOTHIE

Penny Oleksiak
Toronto, ON

Credit: Kat Rizza

Olympic Medallist in Swimming

SERVINGS 2 / PREPARATION 15 MIN / COOKING 5 MIN

INGREDIENTS

Eggs & Guac

	Butter
2	eggs
½	avocado
15 ml (1 tbsp)	salsa (mild or spicy)
2	slices of bread
	Mayo, to taste
	Sriracha sauce, to taste
1 pinch	salt

Smoothie

1	frozen banana
125 ml (½ cup)	frozen strawberries
30 ml (2 tbsp)	vanilla Greek yogurt
250 ml (1 cup)	orange juice

PREPARATION

Eggs & Guac

1. Heat the butter in a pan on low-medium heat. Fry the eggs.
2. In a bowl, combine the avocado with 15 ml (1 tbsp) of salsa to make the guacamole.
3. Toast two slices of bread.
4. Put a thin layer of mayo, some sriracha sauce and one fried egg on each slice of toast.
5. Put some guacamole on top of each egg and top off with a pinch of salt.

Smoothie

1. Place the banana and strawberries into the blender.
2. Add Greek yogurt and orange juice.

" *Blend and enjoy!* "

"Is there anything better than the smell of fresh-baked bread and rolls?
My mother's rolls were a favourite of mine and my 16 brothers and sisters.
Try this recipe—I think they'll become a favourite of yours, too."

THERESA MCNEIL'S DINNER ROLLS

**The Honourable
Stephen McNeil**
Upper Granville, NS

Premier of Nova Scotia

SERVINGS 48 / PREPARATION 1 H 15 MIN / COOKING 15 MIN

INGREDIENTS

30 ml (2 tbsp)	instant yeast
1 kg (7–8 cups)	flour separated
	528 g (4 cups) and 396 g (3–4 cups)
125 ml (½ cup)	white sugar
5 ml (1 tsp)	salt
2	eggs lightly beaten
75 ml (⅓ cup)	oil
750 ml (3 cups)	warm water

PREPARATION

Preheat oven to 180°C (350°F)

1. In a large bowl mix together yeast and 528 g (4 cups) of flour; set aside.
2. In a small bowl mix together sugar, salt, eggs, oil and water.
3. Add wet ingredients to the flour mixture stirring together; will be quite wet.
4. Add 396 g (3 cups) of flour. Use your hands to mix, adding more flour if needed. **Hint:** grease your hands prior to mixing.
5. Continue until mixture is no longer sticky and forms a ball.
6. Leaving in the mixing bowl, cover with a towel and place on top of the stove or other warm place. Let rise 15–20 minutes, punch the dough, return to a warm place.
7. Repeat this process two more times.
8. Divide dough into smaller balls, place in well greased 22 x 32-cm (9 x 13–inch) pans.
9. Let rise 1 hour and then bake 15–20 minutes until golden brown.
10. When removed from the oven, put a little butter on waxed paper and rub the tops of the rolls.
11. Place on a wire rack to cool.

 "In Nova Scotia, you can visit Canada's oldest National Historic Site in Annapolis Royal, take a stroll on the beautiful Halifax waterfront or play golf at world-class golf courses on Cape Breton Island."

"This is a family recipe created on the shores of Lac-Saint-Jean. I often prepare it with trout freshly caught by my father, who returns from fishing while the whole family is gathered at the cottage."

TROUT MOUSSE

Marianne St-Gelais
Saint-Félicien, QC

Olympic Medallist in Speed Skating

SERVINGS 24 / PREPARATION 10 MIN / COOKING 10 MIN

INGREDIENTS

250 g (9 oz)	fresh trout (ideally) or 1 can of trout or salmon
250 g (9 oz)	Philadelphia cream cheese
1	splash of olive oil
	Salt and pepper
	Cilantro, to taste
	Crackers

PREPARATION

1. Clean the fresh trout and cook as desire. Let cool.
2. Remove the skin and bones.
3. In a food processor, add the trout, cheese, oil, salt and pepper, blend.
4. Transfer to a serving bowl; add cilantro.
5. Serve on crackers.

"My favourite place in Canada is the 'Véloroute des Bleuets', Quebec. It's a wonderful way to discover the Saguenay–Lac-Saint-Jean area while exercising!"

"This is my secret (but not so secret anymore) family turkey stuffing recipe. It is always the biggest hit at holiday dinners and reminds me of my mom every time I make it."

TURKEY STUFFING

Terri Clark
Medicine Hat, AB

Country Music Artist

SERVINGS 8–10 / PREPARATION 15 MIN

INGREDIENTS

227 g (1 cup)	butter, melted
1	medium onion, chopped
2	celery stalks, chopped
45 ml (3 tbsp)	fresh sage, chopped
60 ml (4 tbsp)	fresh thyme, chopped
	Salt and pepper
3–4 good dashes	poultry seasoning, to taste
1.5 L (6 cups)	bread cubes
	Chicken broth
1–2 dashes	savoury seasoning for added flavour

PREPARATION

1. If you are using fresh bread, break it into pieces and spread it on a baking sheet. Place it in the oven at low temperature, to harden.
2. Chop the onion and celery in place in a microwavable dish.
3. Add the butter, salt, pepper, sage, thyme and poultry seasoning.
4. Microwave 4–5 minutes until the onions and celery are soft and the butter is melted.
5. Place the bread crumbs in a large mixing bowl, add the onion/celery mixture and enough chicken broth to moisten the mixture.
6. Add seasoning, to taste.
7. If it is too moist and the bread is sticking together, bake it at 180°F (350°C) until golden and crispy.

"My favourite places are the Rockies, Lake Louise and Vancouver Island. My current personal favourite: the Great Lakes and Southern Ontario area. I love to spend the summers at my cottage in Norfolk County."

"My wife and I love cooking this simple recipe. This bread is perfect for breakfast with café au lait or tea."

ZUCCHINI AND WALNUT BREAD

Alain Bouchard
Chicoutimi, QC

Founder and Executive Chairman of the Board,
Alimentation Couche-Tard & Circle K Convenience Stores

SERVINGS 10–12 / PREPARATION 15 MIN / COOKING 60–70 MIN

INGREDIENTS

500 ml (2 cups)	zucchini, finely grated
250 ml (1 cup)	brown sugar
250 ml (1 cup)	vegetable oil
750 ml (3 cups)	all-purpose flour
250 ml (1 cup)	walnuts
3	large eggs
8 ml (1 ½ tsp)	salt
8 ml (1 ½ tsp)	baking soda
8 ml (1 ½ tsp)	baking powder
8 ml (1 ½ tsp)	cinnamon
1.25 ml (¼ tsp)	almond extract

PREPARATION

Preheat oven to 180°C (350°F)

1. In a large bowl, combine the oil, sugar and almond extract.
2. Add the eggs and beat with a food mixer for 10 minutes.
3. Add the zucchini.
4. Add the remaining ingredients.
5. Pour the batter in a bread pan lined with parchment paper.
6. Bake in the oven 60–70 minutes.
7. Let cool on a rack.

*"I like spending evenings on the shore of Lake Archambault in Saint-Donat, Quebec.
It is peaceful and the view is magnificent."*

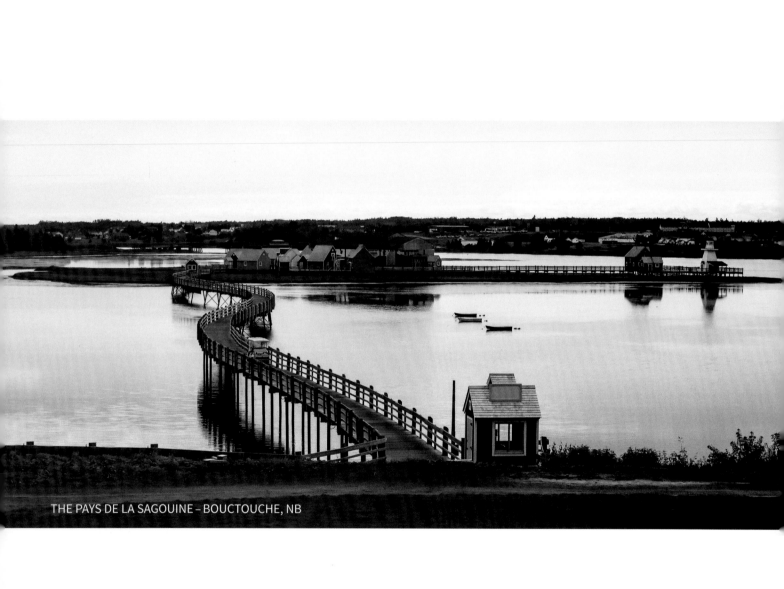

THE PAYS DE LA SAGOUINE – BOUCTOUCHE, NB

APPETIZERS

"This recipe was taken from 'The Saffron Tales', by Yasmin Khan."

CHICK PEAS AND YOGURT SOUP

Joannie Rochette
Montreal, QC

Olympic Medallist in Figure Skating

SERVINGS 6–8 / PREPARATION 30 MIN / COOKING 30 MIN

INGREDIENTS

30 ml (2 tbsp)	butter
30 ml (2 tbsp)	sunflower oil
2	medium onions, finely chopped
3	garlic cloves, minced
500 ml (2 cups)	chick peas, drained, rinsed
1.25 L (5 cups)	chicken or vegetable broth
75 ml (⅓ cup)	rice pudding
500 g (16 oz)	Greek yogurt
60 ml (¼ cup)	chives, finely chopped
15 ml (1 tbsp)	dill, finely chopped (and a bit more for garnish)
30 ml (2 tbsp)	parsley, finely chopped
15 ml (1 tbsp)	dried mint
15 ml (1 tbsp)	corn flour, mixed with 30 ml (2 tbsp) cold water
15 ml (1 tbsp)	sea salt
8 ml (½ tbsp)	ground black pepper

PREPARATION

1. In a saucepan, combine and melt the butter and oil; add the onions and fry for about 5 minutes or until tender and golden.
2. Add the garlic and sauté for 1 minute; add the chick peas, broth and rice. Cook for 10 minutes.
3. Put the yogurt into a large bowl; gradually add a few ladles of warm soup and mix well.
4. Add the herbs, flour mixture, salt and pepper.
5. Add the yogurt mixture to the soup; cook on low heat for 15 minutes stirring occasionally.
6. Adjust the seasoning, to taste.
7. Serve and garnish with dill.

"My favourite place in Canada is the Nouvel-Air Skydiving Centre in Farnham, Quebec."

"This is a recipe I love from 'Chatelaine' magazine and want to share with you."

CILANTRO-LIME CHICKEN SOUP

Clara Hughes
Winnipeg, MA

Credit: Simon Baker

Olympic Medallist in Cycling and Speed Skating

SERVINGS 4–6 / PREPARATION 30 MIN / COOKING 30 MIN

INGREDIENTS

30 ml (2 tbsp)	vegetable oil
15 cm (6 in)	tortilla, cut into bite-sized strips
1	leek, thinly sliced
2	bell peppers, chopped
2	celery stalks, chopped
3	garlic cloves, minced
750 ml (3 cups)	water
15 ml (1 tbsp)	dried oregano
1.25 ml (¼ tsp)	hot red chili flakes
1.25 ml (¼ tsp)	nutmeg
1	chicken bouillon cube
1	skinless, boneless chicken breasts, or thighs, excess fat trimmed, cut in 2–3 pieces
250 ml (1 cup)	frozen corn kernels
½	lime, juiced
125 ml (½ cup)	cilantro, coarsely chopped
1 ½	limes, in wedges

PREPARATION

1. Place a very large wide pot over medium heat. Add 15 ml (1 tbsp) oil. Add tortilla strips. Cook 2–3 minutes, stirring frequently, until toasted. Remove and place on a plate lined with paper towels.
2. Add remaining 15 ml (1 tbsp) to pot. Add the leek. Cook 1 minute, stirring frequently until leek softens slightly.
3. Add peppers and celery. Cook for about 12 minutes until vegetables begin to caramelize.
4. Add garlic and cook for 1 minute.
5. Stir in 750 ml (3 cups) of water and spices. Increase heat to high and bring to a boil. Add a bouillon cube and stir until dissolved.
6. Add the chicken. Reduce heat and simmer for 6 minutes until the chicken is cooked through.
7. Remove chicken, place on a cutting board. Using two forks, shred the meat. Then stir into soup.
8. Add corn. Cook for 2 minutes until corn is hot.
9. Stir in lime juice and add the cilantro.
10. Serve soup with wedges and garnish with tortilla strips.

> *Soup keeps well in the refrigerator for 3 days or in the freezer for 1 month. If making ahead of time, stir in cilantro just before serving.*

"I love to ride my bike in the beautiful Canadian Rockies, around Canmore, where I live."

"My family and I have had the good fortune of enjoying time in the Bahamas over the years, so this little delicious dish takes us right there, even when we can't physically be there."

COCONUT SHRIMP

Melinda Rogers
Toronto, ON

Founder, Rogers Venture Partners,
Vice Chair of Rogers Control Trust

SERVINGS 4 / PREPARATION 15 MIN / COOKING 5 MIN

INGREDIENTS

12	whole raw tiger shrimp
1	egg
125 ml (½ cup)	milk
250 ml (1 cup)	shredded sweetened coconut
125 ml (½ cup)	fine bread crumbs
125 ml (½ cup)	white flour
1 pinch	cayenne pepper, nutmeg and salt
250 ml (1 cup)	frying oil

Garnish

Cocktail sauce
Lemon wedges
Butter lettuce leaves
Parsley, finely chopped

PREPARATION

1. Remove the shell and tail from the shrimp; be sure to remove all traces of the vein and discard.
2. Butterfly the shrimp by cutting along the back of each; pat dry.
3. Add the cayenne pepper, nutmeg and salt to the flour and mix together in a bowl.
4. Whisk the egg and milk together in a second bowl.
5. Mix the coconut and breadcrumbs together in a third bowl.
6. Toss shrimp in the seasoned flour bowl so it is coated evenly on all sides.
7. Dip the coated shrimp in the egg and milk mix bowl, letting excess run off.
8. Place the egg-washed shrimp in the coconut and breadcrumb mix bowl and press down gently, turning over until the shrimp is firmly coated on all sides.
9. Heat oil in a wok and fry the shrimp until golden brown, turning when needed.
10. Place on paper towels to drain excess oil.
11. Serve on a bed of butter lettuce leaves with cocktail sauce and lemon wedges, sprinkle with finely chopped parsley.

 "I have fond memories tapping maple syrup up north with my young sons and look forward to continuing this tradition with them as they grow and mentor their little sister."

"It's simple, I made it up to bring together a lot of stuff that my wife, Donna, likes to eat. You can serve it with any protein that suits your taste."

CRUNCHY SALAD

Colm Feore
Windsor, ON

Actor

SERVINGS 6 / PREPARATION 15 MIN

INGREDIENTS

1	fennel bulb, cored, cut in half; cut each half into three pieces and then slice them into 1 cm (½ in) pieces
2–3	watermelon radishes, cut in bite-sized bits
3–4	red radishes, cut into quarters, sliced
1	cucumber, cut, cored, cubed
1	red bell pepper, cut, cored, cubed
1 head	radicchio, cut into quarters, cored, sliced into 1 cm (½ in) thick shreds
1 head	romaine lettuce, cut in half, sliced into 1 cm (½ in) thick shreds
2	Belgian endives, cut in half, cored, sliced crosswise into 1 cm (½ in) shreds
1	handful of arugula
1	handful of mixed greens
	Toasted pumpkin seeds (optional)
	Maldon salt
	Freshly ground black pepper, to taste
	Extra virgin olive oil
	White balsamic vinegar, to taste (I like Chuck Hughes's version which as he says, adds that wonderful sweet/sour taste without changing the colour of the vegetables.)

PREPARATION

1. Toast a handful of pumpkin seeds in a hot dry pan. Stop when they pop and begin to brown. Remove from pan right away so they do not burn.
2. Place the crunchy vegetables into one salad bowl.
3. Place rest of the greens into a second bowl.
4. Dress them separately by first adding a splash or two of the vinegar and a good pinch of Maldon salt crunched between your fingers. Add a grind or two of pepper to each bowl.
5. Toss both and be sure the vegetables are all lightly dressed with the vinegar. You'll be able to see if they are by the shiny look of the ingredients, but taste to be sure.
6. Now add a splash or two of olive oil to each bowl and toss to cover.

To Serve

1. Arrange a handful of the leafy greens on a bowl or a plate.
2. Spoon the crunchy veg in the centre of same.
3. Sprinkle the toasted pumpkin seeds over the whole, to taste.

"One of my favourite things to do in Canada is check out restaurants with innovative chefs, inspiring the rest of us to try to do better at home. My latest taste experience was at Martin Picard's extraordinary sugar shack outside Montreal."

"Every July our eastern Prince Edward Island community hosts the Village Feast, a rollicking foodie circus, steak dinner for 1,000. It's a local food extravaganza and feel-good fundraiser that benefits our local food banks, puts winter coats on kids and raises enough money to build a school cookhouse in rural Kenya. Perhaps most importantly, it reminds us that we have enough, so much that we can share with another village half a world away.

This hearty nutritious vegetarian dish is a staple in the Kenyan cookhouses we build. To connect the crowd to the cause, we serve it at the Village Feast as well. In Africa, the dish is traditionally made with maize but we've adapted it for Canadian kitchens with yellow corn."

KENYAN GITHERI
(CURRIED KALE & CORN STEW)

Michael Smith
Fortune Bridge, PEI

Celebrity Chef

SERVINGS 4–6 / PREPARATION 15 MIN / COOKING 10 MIN

INGREDIENTS

15 ml (1 tbsp)	vegetable oil
1	large freshly onion, chopped
3	cloves of freshly minced garlic
15 ml (1 tbsp)	curry powder
796 ml (28 oz)	diced tomatoes or fresh tomatoes, chopped
750 g (1.5 lb)	frozen corn or 4 cups of fresh corn
540 ml (19 oz)	cooked beans, drained, rinsed (canned)
3 ml (½ tsp)	salt
Plenty	freshly ground pepper
1	large bunch of fresh kale, chopped

PREPARATION

1. Splash the oil into a small pot over medium-high heat then toss in the onions and garlic. Cook, stirring frequently, with heat high enough to sizzle but not high enough to scorch, lightly browning, softening textures and brightening the flavours of the aromatic vegetables; just 3–4 minutes.

2. Sprinkle in the curry powder and stir for a moment or two to brighten its spice and flavour.

3. Pour in the tomatoes, corn and beans. Season with salt and pepper, to taste.

4. Briefly bring the works to a full, furious boil then immediately reduce to a slow, steady simmer.

5. Stir in the kale and cook until tender and bright green.

6. Serve and share!

" Food is universal. Every time we enjoy this dish, I'm able to remind my family that this is how other families eat. It's a delicious reminder that food connects us all. "

 "I love visiting Newfoundland and go to Mallard Cottage for one of the most authentic food experiences on the planet."

"While I was living in Mexico in the early 1970s, I had the opportunity to immerse myself in the culinary culture of this beautiful country. The Mexican shrimp dish has been one of my favourite dishes, which I served to my friends, who always inquired about the recipe."

MEXICAN SHRIMP

Lise Watier
Montreal, QC

Entrepreneur

SERVINGS 8 / PREPARATION 15 MIN

INGREDIENTS

24	large shrimps, cooked (fresh or frozen), hulled
625 ml (2 ½ cups)	ripe tomatoes, diced
625 ml (2 ½ cups)	white onions, diced or finely chopped
1–2	jalapeño chili pepper(s), finely chopped, to taste
2	garlic cloves, minced
125 ml (½ cup)	fresh lime juice
125 ml (½ cup)	extra virgin olive oil
5 ml (1 tsp)	*Tajín seasoning
	Salt and pepper
1 package	cilantro, leaves and stems, chopped
	Avocado slices (to garnish)

PREPARATION

1. Combine all ingredients, except the avocado and cilantro in a large mixing bowl.
2. Marinate in an airtight container or large Ziploc bag in the fridge for 48 hours, turning the container or bag from time to time so the liquid coats all ingredients.
3. Just before serving, add the cilantro and mix well.
4. Adjust seasoning, to taste.
5. Serve with one or two slices of avocado and some corn chips.

" *Tajín is a Mexican seasoning made of chili peppers, lime juice and salt. "

"I very much like the Park restaurant in Westmount, Montreal. They serve current and very healthy Japanese food. I love the chef, who always cooks special dishes for me. The atmosphere is casual. I also love another local restaurant, Milos, for their fresh fish dishes. It is a local institution: I've been going to this restaurant for nearly thirty years. Finally, when I'm in the mood for French cuisine, I love going to Toqué, a restaurant in Old Montreal."

"It's always a big hit and I've been making it since the '70s."

MY FAMOUS CAESAR SALAD

Jeanne Beker
Toronto, ON

Fashion Journalist, Editor and Author

SERVINGS 6 / PREPARATION 10 MIN

INGREDIENTS

Dressing

125 ml (½ cup)	vegetable or canola oil
30 ml (2 tbsp)	lemon juice
30 ml (2 tbsp)	Worcestershire sauce
2	garlic cloves, crushed
5 ml (1 tsp)	Dijon mustard
15 ml (1 tbsp)	red wine vinegar
5 ml (1 tsp)	dried oregano
1 ml (¼ tsp)	black pepper
1 tin	anchovies, mashed
1	egg yolk

Other ingredients

2	heads of romaine lettuce, use mainly hearts and inner leaves
125 ml (½ cup)	Parmesan cheese, grated

PREPARATION

1. Combine dressing ingredients except for egg yolk and mix well.
2. Stir in one egg yolk just before serving.
3. Toss with the romaine lettuce and Parmesan cheese.

"I've loved beluga watching in the Arctic, shopping at the Lunenberg Folk Art Festival in Nova Scotia, visiting my daughter in the Yukon, just outside of Dawson City and attending the Warkworth Maple Syrup Festival, in my neighbourhood in Northumberland County, Ontario."

"This is the meal I like to cook when I have friends coming over to my Los Angeles home. The atmosphere is convivial and everyone can help themselves directly from the stove. I also cook it occasionally for my family for Christmas."

RED LENTIL SOUP

Daniel Lanois
Gatineau, QC

Musician and Producer

SERVINGS 6 / PREPARATION 15 MIN / COOKING 10 MIN

INGREDIENTS

125 ml (½ cup)	carrots, sliced
125 ml (½ cup)	onions, diced
1	garlic clove, minced (optional)
1	bay leaf
10 ml (2 tsp)	olive oil
5 ml (1 tsp)	ground turmeric
5 ml (1 tsp)	Garam Masala
15 ml (1 tbsp)	fresh lemon juice
1	small jalapeno chili pepper
500 ml (2 cups)	red lentils
2–3	tomatoes peeled, seeded, diced
1.5—2 L (6–8 cups)	chicken broth, ideally homemade
	Salt and pepper

PREPARATION

1. In a large saucepan, add olive oil and sauté the vegetables until tender.
2. Add the broth, lentils and all spices.
3. Cover, bring to a boil and simmer until the lentils are soft.
4. Add more chicken broth if necessary.
5. Remove from heat and add lemon juice.
6. Serve in large bowls with plain yogurt.

" *Sometimes, I add cooked chicken pieces.* "

"When I'm home, I enjoy shooting a good game of pool with friends."

"This is my father-in-law's recipe.
This soup was served to me when I had my first meal with my wife's family."

SAGUENAY—LAC-SAINT-JEAN BROAD BEAN SOUP

Pierre Lavoie
Anse-Saint-Jean, QC

Athlete, Co-founder of
Le Grand Défi Pierre Lavoie and Speaker

SERVINGS 12 / PREPARATION 15 MIN / COOKING 3 H

INGREDIENTS

625 ml (2 ½ cups)	broad beans, or fava beans, shelled
3.5 L (12–15 cups)	water
60 ml (¼ cup)	Bovril liquid beef bouillon or a 375 g (1 ½ lb) beef shank
340 g (¾ lb)	salted pork belly
1	large onion, chopped
6	small carrots, cut into slices
125 ml (½ cup)	yellow beans, chopped
180 ml (¾ cup)	barley
	Salt and pepper
284 ml (10 oz)	corn (optional)

PREPARATION

1. Place all ingredients in a large saucepan.
2. Bring to a boil and simmer for 3 hours, or until the beans are tender and brown.

❝ *Serve and enjoy!* ❞

"The most beautiful village in Canada is my native village, l'Anse-Saint-Jean."

"A family favourite, created by experimenting with existing recipes."

SASKATCHEWAN CHICKPEA SALAD

The Honourable Brad Wall
Swift Current, SK

Premier of Saskatchewan

SERVINGS 4–6 / PREPARATION 15 MIN

INGREDIENTS

Salad

940 ml (32 oz)	chickpeas, drained, rinsed
60 ml (¼ cup)	fresh parsley, chopped
150 ml (⅔ cup)	bell peppers, mix red, yellow and orange, chopped
1	English cucumber, chopped
180 ml (¾ cup)	grape tomatoes, halved
60 ml (¼ cup)	purple onion, chopped
12	Kalamata olives, sliced in half
75 ml (⅓ cup)	feta cheese, crumbled

Dressing

60 ml (¼ cup)	extra virgin olive oil
30 ml (2 tbsp)	Greek yogurt
15 ml (1 tbsp)	freshly squeezed lemon juice
15 ml (1 tbsp)	red wine vinegar
1	small garlic clove, minced
	Salt and pepper

PREPARATION

1. In a large bowl, toss together the salad ingredients.
2. In a separate bowl, whisk together the dressing ingredients.
3. Pour the dressing over the salad and toss, then refrigerate for at least 1 hour before serving.
4. To serve, transfer to serving bowl and squeeze more fresh lemon juice over salad.
5. Garnish with lemon slices.

"What I love about Canada are the Cypress Hills, Saskatchewan's beautiful incongruity, a mountainous formation rising suddenly out of the prairies. Cypress is a forested oasis, peaceful, steeped in history, a place where one feels blessed to be a Canadian."

"It was my nonna's recipe, handed over to my mom, and now I make it."

STRACCIATELLA SOUP

Rick Campanelli
Hamilton, ON

Co-Host, Entertainment Tonight Canada

SERVINGS 6 / PREPARATION 10 MIN / COOKING 8 MIN

INGREDIENTS

1.5 L (6 cups)	chicken broth
	Salt and ground pepper
3	large eggs
30 ml (2 tbsp)	parsley, chopped
250 ml (1 cup)	baby spinach or more, to taste
30 ml (2 tbsp)	both Parmesan and Romano cheeses

PREPARATION

1. Bring chicken broth to a simmer.
2. Whisk together the eggs, Parmesan cheese, parsley and salt/pepper.
3. Slowly pour the egg mixture into the broth while stirring.
4. Continue to stir until the eggs are set, about 1 minute.
5. Add baby spinach and stir to wilt.
6. Sprinkle even more Parmesan and Romano cheeses, if you like cheese.

" *Serve immediately!* "

"I love taking my family for a bike ride along Toronto's waterfront bike trail, then head home for a barbecue followed by a visit to our local ice cream shop."

"I wanted to make a recipe that really showcased the unique flavour and uses for SUNSET® Campari® tomatoes. By cooking the Campari®, I can showcase how their flavour profile develops and changes in new ways, it's a totally different experience from eating them raw which is equally as amazing."

SUNSET® CAMPARI® TOMATO GALETTE

Roger Mooking
Toronto, ON

Food Network Canada and
Cooking Channel Canada Host

SERVINGS 4–6 / PREPARATION 50 MIN / COOKING 35–40 MIN

INGREDIENTS

375 ml (1 ½ cups)	unbleached all-purpose flour
2 ml (½ tsp)	ground black peppercorns
2 ml (½ tsp)	kosher salt
2 ml (½ tsp)	dried oregano
125 ml (½ cup)	cubed unsalted butter, room temperature
180 ml (¾ cup)	cold water
5	SUNSET® Campari® tomatoes
2 ml (½ tsp)	fresh rosemary, finely chopped
5 ml (1 tsp)	fresh thyme, finely chopped
30 ml (2 tbsp)	breadcrumbs
60 ml (¼ cup)	Parmesan cheese, grated
1	large egg, beaten

PREPARATION

Preheat oven to 190°C (375°F)

Dough

1. Mix all dry ingredients so they are evenly combined.
2. Crumble the butter into the dry ingredients using your fingertips only until pea-sized crumbs form. Refrigerate for 10 minutes.
3. Using the handle side of a wooden spoon, mix cold water into the flour mixture until it comes together.
4. Using your hand, gently knead the dough into a disc.
5. Refrigerate dough 10–15 minutes.

Garnish

1. Slice Campari® tomatoes to 0.5 cm (¼ in) thickness with a very sharp knife and set aside.
2. In a separate bowl, combine rosemary and thyme together. Set aside.

Assembly

1. On a clean surface lightly dusted with all-purpose flour, roll out dough to 25 cm (10 in) circle. Thin the outer 2.5 cm (1 in) of the circle so there is a thinner border.
2. Carefully transfer circle to a parchment lined baking tray. Refrigerate for 10 minutes.
3. In the centre of the dough, spread the breadcrumbs and leave a 2.5 cm (1 in) border uncovered.
4. Sprinkle half of the Parmesan cheese on top of the breadcrumbs.
5. Starting from the centre, place the tomato slices in concentric circles, overlapping each slice by half, making sure the tomatoes cover the edge of the Parmesan cheese-breadcrumb mixture.
6. Sprinkle a pinch of ground black peppercorn and the mixed herbs over the tomatoes. Sprinkle remaining Parmesan cheese over the top of the tomatoes.
7. Lift the edges of the dough and fold them inward over the filling, pleating as you go, to create a folded-over border.
8. Brush edge of galette with beaten egg.
9. Bake in preheated oven 35–40 minutes, rotating pan halfway through. The edges of the dough should be browned and the dough cooked fully through.
10. Allow the galette to rest for 10 minutes then transfer to a service board.
11. Serve warm with Crème Fraîche.

"Canada has embraced diversity for generations, and the incredible benefits of this mélange come together in a way that is unprecedented in the world. I can experience authentic food that I've had on my travels right in my back yard."

"This recipe comes from my mother, who knows what winter needs are."

THE FINEST GIFT FROM THE UNFAIRLY DISPARAGED PARSNIP (SOUP)

David Walmsley
Toronto, ON

Editor in Chief, The Globe and Mail

SERVINGS 4–6 / PREPARATION 5 MIN / COOKING 40 MIN

INGREDIENTS

30 ml (2 tbsp)	butter
1	large onion, chopped
1–2 pinches	curry powder
454 g (1 lb)	parsnips, cut up
1 L (4 cups)	chicken or vegetable broth

PREPARATION

1. In a saucepan, cook the onion in melted butter. Cover saucepan to soften, but not brown, the onions.
2. Add one teaspoon of curry powder, the parsnips and the chicken or vegetable broth.
3. Cover and let simmer for 40 minutes, or until parsnips soften.
4. Liquidize or blend, until as smooth as required.

" *Reheat before serving if necessary. Enjoy!* "

"What I enjoy most about Canada is absorbing all the seasons in Algonquin Park, Ontario, especially snowshoeing around Jack Lake."

"I called it Water Ramp Salad because it's the salad my mom used to make for me during my water ramp training camps."

WATER RAMP SALAD

Mikaël Kingsbury
Deux-Montagnes, QC

Olympic Medallist in Moguls Skiing

SERVINGS 2–3 / PREPARATION 30 MIN / COOKING 10 MIN

INGREDIENTS

12	cherry tomatoes
125 ml (½ cup)	olive oil
3	garlic cloves, chopped
1	bunch fresh basil, chopped
10 ml (2 tsp)	sea salt
5 ml (1 tsp)	balsamic vinegar
2	jalapeno peppers, chopped
300 g (10 oz)	pasta al dente

PREPARATION

1. Combine the garlic, jalapeno peppers, basil, balsamic vinegar, olive oil and sea salt in a bowl.
2. Marinate in the refrigerator 3–4 hours.
3. Add pasta, tomatoes and serve.

" *Very good with black olives.* "

 "I love the mountains of Western Canada. They're a skier's paradise!
I also like the Montreal Canadiens Bell Centre!"

MORAINE LAKE – BANFF NATIONAL PARK, AB

ENTREES

"From my mom's 'Fannie Farmer Boston Cooking-School Cook Book', which every year wears a little more Hollandaise sauce."

ALBERTA ROAST BEEF AND YORKSHIRE PUDDING WITH HOLLANDAISE COVERED BROCCOLI

The Honourable Rachel Notley
Fairview, AB

Premier of Alberta

SERVINGS 8–10 / PREPARATION 45 MIN / COOKING 1 H 30 MIN

INGREDIENTS

2 kg (4 lb)	roast beef
	Salt and pepper
1	broccoli, steamed

Yorkshire Pudding

4	eggs
250 ml (1 cup)	milk
3 ml (½ tsp)	salt
250 ml (1 cup)	flour
	Butter

Hollandaise Sauce

3	eggs
10 ml (2 tsp)	lemon juice or mild vinegar
125 ml (½ cup)	butter or margarine, melted
3 ml (½ tsp)	salt
15 ml (1 tbsp)	water, approximately
	Grains of cayenne, to taste

PREPARATION

Roast Beef

Preheat oven to 160°C (325°F)

1. In a large skillet over medium–high heat, brown the roast on all sides. Season with salt and pepper.
2. Roast at 160°C (325°F) for about 75 minutes, then cover.
3. Continue cooking until a meat thermometer inserted into the centre of the roast reads 48°C (118°F) for rare doneness.
4. Remove the roast and let it rest for 10 minutes.

Yorkshire Pudding

Preheat oven to 230°C (450°F)

1. Mix 4 eggs with milk and 3 ml (½ tsp) of salt.
2. Add flour and mix together.
3. Add 3 ml (½ tsp or less) of butter into each cupcake tin and heat in oven until bubbling.
4. Add Yorkshire pudding mix to each cupcake tin and bake 20–25 min.
5. Serve with roast beef.

Hollandaise Sauce

1. Put 3 eggs in a small heavy saucepan or double boiler top.
2. Beat with a wooden spoon or wire whisk until smooth but not fluffy.
3. Add lemon juice or mild vinegar, butter, water, salt and few grains of cayenne.
4. Set over very low heat or hot water and beat until the sauce begins to thicken, about 5 minutes. The sauce will thicken as it cools. Makes about 250 ml (1 cup).
5. Serve over steamed broccoli.

"My favourite festival is the Edmonton Folk Fest, but as an everyday favourite place I'd choose Edmonton's River Valley and the gravel running trails right along the North Saskatchewan River."

"This recipe is a modified West Coast favourite."

BAKED BC SOCKEYE SALMON WITH MORNAY SAUCE

The Honourabl Christy Clark
Vancouver, BC

Premier of British Columbia
(2011~2017)

SERVINGS 4 / PREPARATION 30 MIN / COOKING 10 MIN

INGREDIENTS

4	BC sockeye salmon fillets, serving size
5 ml (1 tsp)	extra virgin olive oil
5 ml (1 tsp)	lemon juice
5 ml (1 tsp)	dried dill

Mornay Sauce

45 ml (3 tbsp)	butter
45 ml (3 tbsp)	all-purpose flour
500 ml (2 cups)	warmed milk
2 ml (¼ tsp)	kosher salt
1 ml (⅛ tsp)	white pepper
1 pinch	freshly grated nutmeg
60 ml (¼ cup)	grated strong cheese, such as Gruyere or old white cheddar

PREPARATION

Preheat the oven to 230°C (450°F)

1. In a shallow open casserole dish, brush a thin layer of olive oil.
2. Place fillets on top of the oil, skin side down.
3. Brush each fillet with lemon juice and sprinkle on some of the dill. Bake for 8 minutes.

Mornay Sauce

1. Warm the milk in the microwave and set aside.
2. In a medium saucepan, melt the butter over medium heat.
3. Slowly add the flour and cook, stirring constantly, until the roux is pale yellow and frothy. Do not allow the roux to brown.
4. Slowly whisk in the warmed milk and continue to whisk until the sauce thickens and comes to a light boil, 2–4 minutes.
5. Reduce the heat to a simmer and season with salt, white pepper and nutmeg.
6. Allow to simmer for 2 more minutes. Briskly stir in the grated cheese until melted.
7. Place a baked fillet of salmon on each plate; spoon some Mornay sauce on each and drizzle with a bit of the remaining dried dill.

❝ *Serve with a nice mixture of cooked colourful vegetables. Bon Appetit!* ❞

"Canada has it all! We have clean air, fresh water, mountains, lakes, rivers, valleys and plains. Great small towns and great cities too. We have breathtaking scenery, a wonderfully diverse multicultural population, innovative thinkers, entrepreneurs, inventors, great artists, painters, writers, poets, researchers, and so much more. Congratulations to all Canadians for helping to make our country so great!"

"This is my father Gilbert's recipe. He used to call it 'his macaroni' but he always used fusilli pasta. He would tell everyone about his macaroni, letting them believe he often cooked for his family. In reality, he only cooked for us twice, but both times, he prepared this recipe with fusilli pasta. Today, when I recall and share this memory, it still makes me smile."

BEEF MAC & CHEESE

Martin Picard
Montreal, QC

Chef, Author and Television Personality

SERVINGS 8 / PREPARATION 30 MIN / COOKING 40 MIN

INGREDIENTS

Sauce

	Cooking oil
2	large onions, minced
1 kg (2 lb)	ground beef
	Salt and pepper
2.5 ml (½ tsp)	ground cloves
2.5 ml (½ tsp)	ground cinnamon
680 ml (2 ¾ cups)	tomato juice

Other

1 L (4 cups)	mozzarella cheese, grated
	Velveeta cheese, sliced, enough to cover the dish
500 g (16 oz)	macaroni

PREPARATION

Preheat oven to 160°C (325°F)

Sauce

1. In a saucepan, heat oil and sauté the onions; season with salt and pepper, to taste.
2. When the onions are golden, add the meat and cook through.
3. Add cinnamon, cloves, salt and pepper.
4. Add tomato juice and reduce by half.

Pasta

1. Heat a saucepan full of salted water.
2. Once the water boils, add the pasta. They are ready when al dente.
3. Drain and place in a baking dish.

Assembly

1. Add the sauce to the pasta, to the edge of the dish.
2. Add mozzarella cheese and mix well. Add pepper, to taste.
3. Cover with Velveeta cheese slices.
4. Bake in the oven for 40 minutes.
5. Brown under the boiler.
6. Serve with a splash of olive oil.

 "The Gaspé Peninsula is one of the most beautiful places in the world. The city of Gaspé and the Saint-Jean River hold my most precious memories. It is also in this area that my kids caught their first salmon."

*"Recipe from 'The Spice Cookbook' by Avanelle Day and Lillie Stuckey.
David White Company, New York, 1964."*

BEEF VINDALOO (INDIAN DISH)

Robert Munsch
Guelph, ON

Storyteller and Author

SERVINGS 4–6 / PREPARATION 15 MIN / COOKING 50–60 MIN

INGREDIENTS

15 ml (1 tbsp)	ground coriander seeds
3 ml (½ tsp)	ground cumin seeds
5 ml (1 tsp)	ground turmeric
3 ml (½ tsp)	powdered mustard
3 ml (½ tsp)	ground red pepper
5 ml (1 tsp)	ground black pepper
3 ml (½ tsp)	ground ginger
30 ml (2 tbsp)	cider vinegar
1 kg (2 lb)	lean shoulder of beef
45 ml (3 tbsp)	onion flakes
1 ml (¼ tsp)	instant minced garlic
45 ml (3 tbsp)	cold water
30 ml (2 tbsp)	butter, margarine, or cooking oil
625 ml (2 ½ cups)	hot water
8 ml (1 ½ tsp)	salt
30 ml (2 tbsp)	fresh lemon juice
	Basmati rice, for serving

PREPARATION

1. Combine first 8 ingredients into a paste; set aside.
2. Trim and discard fat from beef.
3. Cut the meat into 1.25 cm (½ in) pieces; set aside.
4. Rehydrate onion and garlic in cold water, and sauté in butter, margarine or cooking oil.
5. Add the spice paste (made from first 8 ingredients) to the butter mixture; cook 1–2 minutes.
6. Add the meat; cook 10 minutes.
7. Add hot water and let it cook until tender, 40–50 minutes.
8. Add salt and lemon juice.
9. Serve over rice.

"I have visited many places throughout all of Canada. It is all beautiful. I really like the Far North."

"This recipe is my friend Cindy's. She finally revealed it to me after many requests."

BEER AND LEMON SHORT RIBS

Alain Vigneault
Quebec City, QC

NHL Head Coach

SERVINGS 2 / PREPARATION 15 MIN / COOKING 2 H 30

INGREDIENTS

2	racks baby back ribs
	Club House
	Montreal Chicken Seasoning
3	lemons, thinly sliced
1 ½	bottle of brown beer
250 ml (1 cup)	President's Choice
	Smokin' Stampede
	Beer & Chipotle Barbecue Sauce

PREPARATION

Preheat the oven to 180°C (350°F)

1. Peel away the white membrane on the back of the ribs.
2. Rub seasoning thoroughly into the meat on all sides.
3. Lay the racks in a baking dish, meat side down.
4. Cover the ribs with lemon slices.
5. Pour the beer in the bottom of the dish without spilling on seasoning.
6. Cover hermetically with foil.
7. Bake 2–2.5 hours until meat is easily detached from bones.
8. Remove lemon slices.
9. Take 250 ml (1 cup) of the cooking juice and mix with the barbecue sauce.
10. Using a brush, spread the mixture over the ribs.
11. Sear on the barbecue at medium-high heat.

" Serve with Caesar-style potato salad. "

"When I come back home in the summer, I like to wander around the grounds of the Outaouais golf courses and spend time with my friends. It's my summer treat after all the long winter days working in professional hockey."

"This recipe seems to be a 'Muskoka' cottage tradition."

BEER CAN CHICKEN

Brian Orser
Toronto, ON

Olympic Medallist in Figure Skating

SERVINGS 2–4 / PREPARATION 20 MIN / COOKING 1 H 15 MIN

INGREDIENTS

1	whole chicken
½	can of beer
60 ml (¼ cup)	paprika
60 ml (¼ cup)	coarse salt
60 ml (¼ cup)	brown sugar
	Oil

PREPARATION

1. Rinse chicken with cold water and dry with paper towel, rub some oil on the chicken.
2. Mix the paprika, salt and sugar together in a bowl.
3. Rub the mixture on the outside of the chicken, in the cavity and place 15 ml (1 tbsp) in the can of beer.
4. Preheat one side of a barbecue on medium heat.
5. Insert the can of beer in the bottom of the chicken (yes, the bum!) and keep the legs forward.
6. On the non-heat side of the barbecue, place the chicken on a tray to collect drippings and stand it like a tripod.
7. Close lid and cook for 1 hour. Check frequently to ensure the chicken has not tipped over and rotate for even cooking.

" *Perfect at the cottage… enjoy!* **"**

WINE PAIRING

SUE-ANN STAFF ESTATE WINERY
RIESLING LOVED BY LU
VQA NIAGARA PENINSULA

"Speaking of the cottage… This is my favourite place on the planet… Muskoka is peaceful, relaxing and a typical Canadian way of summer life. Traffic is also a way of life going to and from… however, it is worth it!"

"This recipe comes from the Pacific or Atlantic sand bars."

BEER COCKLES

Kevin Parent
Montreal, QC

Singer and Songwriter

INGREDIENTS

1	large saucepan full cockles, clams or soft-shell clams
1	beer

PREPARATION

1. In a large saucepan, add the cockles and beer.
2. Cover and bring to a boil. Boil until the shells open.

" *Enjoy!* "

 "My Canadian favourites are Charlevoix goat cheese and grain fed chicken. Charlevoix is a place I like very much. It is beautiful and abounds with delicacies."

"I used to cook this recipe in my first restaurant in Verdun, Quebec (Simple Chic). It was very popular. It was inspired by the veal chuck roast my mother used to cook for us, and still does to this day, every Sunday evening."

BRAISED VEAL CHEEKS

Louis-François Marcotte
Montreal, QC

Chef and Entrepreneur

SERVINGS 4 / PREPARATION 20 MIN / COOKING 2–3 H

INGREDIENTS

12	veal cheeks
250 ml (1 cup)	bacon, diced
8	garlic cloves, minced
1 bottle	red wine
4 sprigs	of thyme and rosemary
	Freshly ground salt and pepper, to taste
250 ml (1 cup)	green beans
12	ratte potatoes, halved
	Olive oil
2	shallots, chopped
500 ml (2 cups)	young arugula
180 ml (¾ cup)	15% cream

PREPARATION

Preheat oven to 160°C (325°F)

1. Lightly trim the fat off the meat; salt and pepper both sides.
2. Over high heat, sear the cheeks on each side in a skillet to collect the juices from the meat.
3. Remove the meat from the skillet and set it aside.
4. Add the bacon and garlic to the skillet and sauté both until golden brown.
5. Add the cheeks back to the skillet and deglaze with red wine. Add enough wine to cover the veal. Add water if necessary.
6. Add the thyme and rosemary, cover with foil and bake 2–3 hours. Cooking is complete when the meat comes off easily with a fork.
7. Remove the veal from the oven and wrap with foil. Let rest for at least 20 minutes.
8. Meanwhile, reduce the broth by half; the sauce must be shiny.
9. In a skillet, brown the potatoes and shallots. Add the green beans and sauté.
10. Once cooked, add the arugula. Add cream to the sauce so it becomes velvety. Serve.

"Activities, addresses and organizations are as numerous as fabulous in Quebec. I suggest we all take the time to choose carefully and buy Quebec products. I have a little weakness for maple products and 'La Tablée des Pionniers'."

*"This recipe was passed to me by my wife Jennifer a few years ago and
it's such an AMAZING steak that I have to share. She was given this recipe by longtime family friends."*

CANYON'S STEAK

George Canyon
Calgary, AB

Country Singer

SERVING 1 / PREPARATION 15 MIN / COOKING 10 MIN

INGREDIENTS

1	AAA grade Alberta steak (I prefer a nice and thick cut)
30 ml (2 tbsp)	The Keg steak seasoning
30 ml (2 tbsp)	virgin olive oil

PREPARATION

1. Naturally thaw the steak, if frozen.
2. Cover both sides with oil; rub in steak seasoning.
3. Heat barbecue burner to searing hot.
4. Set timer at 2 minutes maximum and place steak on barbecue. Cook both sides for 2 minutes each.
5. Remove steak and allow to cool to room temperature.
6. When cooled, place steak back on barbecue at medium to high heat for approximately 3 minutes each side for medium rare, depending on steak thickness.

"I have the best job in the world as I get to travel this amazing country playing music for my fans. I have been very blessed to visit almost every inch of Canada and it is the most diverse and beautiful country I have ever seen. I love skiing and snowboarding with my family in the rocky mountains and flying my airplane over the gorgeous prairies and foothills. As a proud Canadian that lives at home in Canada I can confidently say that the people that make up this great nation, make this nation GREAT."

"This is common Croatian and Serbian street food.
It's a family recipe, everyone makes it and grew up eating it. It must be 100 years old."

CHEESE BURRAC

Claudia Bunce
Jade City, BC

Credit: Michael J. Hall

Star of Discovery Series JADE FEVER

SERVINGS 8 / PREPARATION 20 MIN / COOKING 45 MIN

INGREDIENTS

454 g (1 lb)	phyllo pastry
125 ml (½ cup)	melted butter
6	eggs
500 ml (2 cups)	cottage cheese
500 ml (2 cups)	feta cheese
60 ml (¼ cup)	sour cream or Kajmak (Croatian cream cheese)

PREPARATION

Preheat oven to 180°C (350°F)

1. Follow defrost instructions on phyllo pastry.
2. Brush 22 x 33–cm (9 x 13–inch) cake pan with melted butter.
3. In a large bowl, whisk the eggs lightly.
4. Break feta cheese apart into small crumbs and add to the egg mixture.
5. Add all cottage cheese and sour cream to egg mixture. Mix until all ingredients are combined.
6. Open phyllo pastry as needed, and then close the package again so the remainder doesn't dry out.
7. Working quickly, put 3 pieces of phyllo onto baking sheet, one at a time; lightly butter in between each sheet.
8. Using a soup ladle, sprinkle one full spoon of cheese mixture on to the top layer of phyllo.
9. Add another sheet of phyllo pastry and brush with butter adding a ladle of egg mixture. Continue layering with one sheet of phyllo pastry and a ladle of egg mixture until all of the mixture is used up.
10. Add an extra phyllo pastry sheet on top and butter last sheet on top.
11. Bake 45 minutes or until golden-brown and middle feels stable.
12. Let sit 10 minutes until slightly cooled.
13. Serve hot, warm or cold.

" Add your own twist to the recipe with different fillings such as a meat and potato, or a sweet fruit filling! "

"My favourite place in Canada is Jade City. We have four beautiful seasons and we're surrounded by majestic mountains full of jade. My family created Jade City, so to us, this is the best place in Canada."

"This Chicken Florentine recipe is one that my mother has made for me many times and passed along to myself and my sisters because it's always been a favourite of ours. I hope it becomes one of yours too! Enjoy!"

CHICKEN FLORENTINE

Aaron Pritchett
Gabriola Island, BC

Country Singer

SERVINGS 4 / PREPARATION 20 MIN / COOKING 30 MIN

INGREDIENTS

4	chicken breasts
60 ml (¼ cup)	butter, melted
750 ml (3 cups)	mushrooms, sliced
30 ml (2 tbsp)	garlic, minced
284 ml (1 can)	mushroom soup
125 ml (½ cup)	half & half or 15% cream
60 ml (¼ cup)	white wine
30 ml (2 tbsp)	fresh lemon juice
45 ml (3 tbsp)	Parmesan cheese, grated
30 ml (2 tbsp)	Italian seasoning, dried
45 ml (3 tbsp)	spinach, frozen, thawed, squeezed
500 ml (2 cups)	mozzarella cheese, grated
150 ml (⅔ cup)	bacon bits, crispy

PREPARATION

Preheat oven to 200°C (400°F)

1. In a pan, season the chicken to taste with salt and pepper. Brown well in a little butter 5–7 minutes. Set aside.
2. While the chicken marinates, brown the mushrooms in butter 5–7 minutes. Add garlic and sauté 1 minute. Set aside.
3. In a bowl, combine soup, cream, wine, juice, Parmesan cheese and Italian seasoning. Set aside.
4. While chicken and mushrooms are browning, place spinach in a clean tea towel and squeeze out all liquid. Set aside.
5. In a 23 x 33–cm (9 x 13–inch) baking dish, layer spinach, then mushrooms, half sauce, chicken, remaining half of sauce, mozzarella cheese, then bacon bits.
6. Bake until browned, approximately 15–20 minutes.

❝ *Enjoy!* **❞**

"I've traveled far and wide across our amazing country many times over and nothing makes me feel as happy as flying west over the Rocky Mountains, knowing I'm coming home to the southwest of British Columbia. Both hiking and fishing are some things I love to do when I have some downtime from touring. Canada will always be my home!"

*"We call this Chicken in a Hurry because it's very easy and absolutely delicious.
It was created out of necessity—a meal needed to be made and time was short! It's very flexible
(and forgiving) and you can substitute the chicken for turkey or pork. Perfect for folks on the go!"*

Oliver Jones
Little Burgundy (Montreal), QC

Jazz Musician

CHICKEN IN A HURRY

SERVINGS 4 / PREPARATION 15 MIN / COOKING 1 H 30 MIN

INGREDIENTS

4	chicken breasts
1 pouch	dry onion soup
1 can	cranberry sauce with the whole fruits
250 ml (1 cup)	orange juice
125 ml (½ cup)	balsamic salad dressing or any other dressing, not too sweet

PREPARATION

Preheat oven to 180°C (350°F)

1. Mix all ingredients except the chicken.
2. Add the chicken breasts and coat them with the mixture.
3. Put all ingredients in an oven-proof casserole dish, like Pyrex.
4. Cover and bake for 90 minutes.

Invite your best friends and savour this delicious dish. Your guests will think that you spent hours in the kitchen and they will all ask you: 'When can we come back?'

"One of my favourite destinations is the beautiful city of Halifax. Not only are the people warm and welcoming, but the seafood is fresh and I can enjoy my favourite dessert: Nova Scotia Blueberry Grunt. Heaven!"

"Putting together ingredients we loved."

CHICKEN PENNE WITH VEGETABLES AND SUN-DRIED TOMATOES

Catriona Le May Doan, O.C.
Saskatoon, SK

Olympic Medallist in Speed Skating

SERVINGS 10–12 / PREPARATION 20 MIN / COOKING 15 MIN

INGREDIENTS

4	chicken breasts, cut into strips
15 ml (1 tbsp)	olive oil
200 g (7 oz)	sun-dried tomatoes in oil
15 ml (1 tbsp)	crushed garlic
	Chicken spice, to taste
454 g (1 lb)	penne, cooked al dente
1	red pepper, sliced
1	yellow pepper, sliced
1	orange pepper, sliced
1	head of broccoli, cut up
125 ml (½ cup)	fresh basil
125 ml (½ cup)	Greek feta, crumbled

PREPARATION

1. Fry the chicken in a pan with the oil on medium heat. Sprinkle (we sprinkle heavily) chicken with chicken spice and continue cooking until cooked through. Season with salt and pepper, to taste.
2. Empty jar of sun-dried tomatoes, with oil and all contents, into medium-sized pot and turn on med/low; add the garlic and allow it to simmer for 5 minutes.
3. Add peppers and broccoli and let it all simmer until al dente.
4. Add chicken and penne to the vegetables, mix together and turn heat to low.
5. When serving, add fresh basil and crumbled Greek feta.

" *Super easy and healthy, and our family loves it! You can add whatever vegetables you love!* "

"Canada is truly the most beautiful place on earth. One of my favourite things to do is to be out in Invermere, BC during the winter, skating on Lake Windermere. The mountains surround the lake and yet the valley is wide and open and allows a ton of sunshine and light. The Whiteway (as they call the cleared path) goes for many kilometres and there is no greater place to go with my family to enjoy the ice, snow, sun, and views. The dogs run along the path and we skate and enjoy our beautiful Canadian winters."

"Like in many homes on Christmas Eve, my mom used to prepare vol-au vent. Because of the special circumstances, the illuminated Christmas tree and the subdued lighting, in my child's head, this meal was rare and exquisite and I loved it just as much as I loved Christmas. One day, I courageously asked my mom if I could have the same meal for my birthday. Since then, and for over 40 years, she places a steaming plate of delicious vol-au-vent on my birthday table, taking me back to those childhood days."

CHICKEN VOL-AU-VENT

David St-Jacques
Quebec City, QC

Astronaut

SERVINGS 4 / PREPARATION 15 MIN / COOKING 30 MIN

INGREDIENTS

2	chicken thighs
5 ml (1 tsp)	olive oil
5 ml (1 tsp)	butter
125 ml (½ cup)	mushrooms, sliced
1	onion, sliced
125 ml (½ cup)	carrots, sliced, cooked al dente
125 ml (½ cup)	frozen peas
75 ml (⅓ cup)	butter
75 ml (⅓ cup)	flour
250 ml (1 cup)	milk
	Salt and pepper

Other

1 pinch	nutmeg
5 ml (1 tsp)	*Herbes de Provence* (blend of herbs)
	Salt and pepper
	Vol-au-vent puff pastries

PREPARATION

1. In a saucepan, cook the chicken in water; add salt and pepper.
2. Remove chicken from broth; set the broth aside for the sauce.
3. Debone and dice the chicken; set aside.
4. In a large skillet, brown the onion and mushrooms in the olive oil and butter; set aside.
5. In the same skillet, make a roux: melt the butter and add the flour. Cook, and let brown a little.
6. Whisk in the milk and then 250 ml (1 cup) of broth.
7. Add the peas and carrots.
8. Add the nutmeg, *Herbes de Provence*, salt and pepper.
9. Add 500 ml (2 cups) of diced chicken.
10. Add the mushrooms and onion. Mix well and cook a few minutes more, warming all added ingredients.
11. Add mixture in vol-au-vent puff pastries and serve.

" *You can refrigerate the dish, set a beautiful table, go to Midnight Mass, and when you return, warm the dish while the vol-au-vent puff pastries are heating in the oven.* "

 "My favourite place in Canada is the Sutton Natural Park, in the Eastern Townships, Quebec, for its beautiful forest and mountain trails. My love story with this magical place started when I was a kid. My father used to take me there during weekends and maybe that's where I got my liking for expeditions and adventures. I go back as often as I can."

"Brian enjoyed preparing this chili with his daughters when they were little. In the Pallister house, it has been renamed 'Pally's Chili' as the recipe is open to creative interpretation. Some of Brian's favourite changes are to substitute canned brown beans for kidney beans and to add kernel corn, garlic cloves and extra onions." (Esther Pallister, the Premier's wife.)

The Honourable Brian Pallister
Winnipeg, MB

Premier of Manitoba

CHUCK WAGON CHILI

SERVINGS 6 / PREPARATION 15 MIN / COOKING 1 H

INGREDIENTS

750 g (1 ½ lb)	ground beef
500 ml (2 cups)	kidney beans, drained
500 ml (2 cups)	water or beef broth
318 ml (1 ¼ cups)	condensed tomato soup, undiluted
1	large onion, chopped
250 ml (1 cup)	sliced mushrooms
2	medium carrots, sliced
6	hot dogs, cut into bite-size pieces
5 ml (1 tsp)	salt
15 ml (1 tbsp)	chili powder
1.25 ml (¼ tsp)	pepper
	Cheddar cheese, shredded, to taste

PREPARATION

1. In a large saucepan, cook the ground beef over medium heat until no longer pink; drain.
2. Add the remaining ingredients and bring to a boil.
3. Reduce heat, cover and let simmer for 1 hour, stirring occasionally.
4. Serve topped with shredded cheddar cheese.

"In my spare time, I love to hike and bike in Manitoba's pristine, picturesque wilderness. In particular, I enjoy riding my mountain bike in the area near my childhood home of Portage la Prairie, in the rugged Whiteshell region, Riding Mountain National Park, the Interlake and in Manitoba's immense boreal forest. I recently biked the entire portion of the Trans-Canada Trail that lies within Manitoba."

"This recipe is my girlfriend's idea."

COD AND ACCOMPANIMENTS

Alex Harvey
Saint-Ferréol-les-Neiges, QC

Cross-country Skiing World Champion

SERVINGS 2–4 / PREPARATION 30 MIN / COOKING 5–7 MIN

INGREDIENTS

Cod

2	cod fillets
2.5 ml (½ tsp)	onion salt
2.5 ml (½ tsp)	paprika
2.5 ml (½ tsp)	ground coriander
2.5 ml (½ tsp)	smoked sweet paprika
15 ml (1 tbsp)	Mexican chili powder
15 ml (1 tbsp)	brown sugar
30 ml (2 tbsp)	flour
	Salt and pepper

White Sauce

60 ml (¼ cup)	plain yogurt
60 ml (¼ cup)	sour cream or mayonnaise
1	lime, juiced
1	shallot, cut into small sections
	Salt and pepper

Cole Slaw

1 bag	cole slaw or red cabbage, minced
60 ml (¼ cup)	vegetable oil
60 ml (¼ cup)	vinegar (or more… there's never too much!)
30 ml (2 tbsp)	sugar
	Salt and pepper (lots of salt)

Salsa

1	red onion, diced
3–4	tomatoes, diced
1	mango, diced
1 can	corn
	Cilantro, chopped (generous)
2	limes, juiced
	Salt and pepper

Guacamole

Mashed avocados, lime juice, sriracha sauce, salt and pepper

PREPARATION

Cod

1. In a bowl, add all ingredients except the cod fillets and mix well.
3. Pat the fillets dry with paper towel and coat them with mixture.
3. In a skillet, melt lots of butter and brown the fillets.

White Sauce

1. In a bowl, add all ingredients and mix well.

Cole Slaw

1. In a bowl, add all ingredients and mix well.

*Salsa

1. In a bowl, add all ingredients and mix well.

*Guacamole

1. In a bowl add all ingredients and mix well.

" *Prepare ahead of time, if possible, as it is much tastier when it has time to soak! "

"My Canadian favourite is the Quebec-based non-profit Laura Lémerveil. I have been their spokesperson since 2015."

"This meal is a family recipe and covers many generations."

EASY POT ROAST

Rich Little
Ottawa, ON

Entertainer

SERVINGS 6 / PREPARATION 30 MIN / COOKING 2 H

INGREDIENTS

1.5 kg (3 lb)	boneless chuck roast
30 ml (2 tbsp)	olive oil
15 ml (1 tbsp)	Worcestershire sauce
430 ml (14 oz)	beef broth
250 ml (1 cup)	dry red wine
5 ml (1 tsp)	salt
2 ml (¼ tsp)	pepper
5 ml (1 tsp)	dried basil
500 ml (2 cups)	onions, chopped
1 kg (2 lb)	potatoes peeled, cut into 5 cm (2 in) pieces
500 ml (2 cups)	carrots cut into 5 cm (2 in) pieces
60 ml (¼ cup)	flour

PREPARATION

1. Brown meat on all sides in hot oil in a 4 to 6-quart cooking pot with a tight-fitting lid. Drain fat.
2. Remove roast from the pot and set aside.
3. Add onion to the same pot and sauté 5–8 minutes.
4. Mix beef broth, red wine, Worcestershire sauce, salt, pepper and basil in a separate bowl.
5. Put roast back into the pot. Pour mixture over roast and onions and bring to a boil. Reduce heat and simmer, covered, for 1 hour.
6. Add potatoes and carrots to the pot. Raise heat until the liquid is bubbling; reduce heat immediately. Simmer while covered until vegetables are tender; 45–60 minutes.

Gravy

1. Pour out and measure the roast juice, skim off the fat and add enough water to make 375 ml (1 ½ cups) of pan sauce.
2. In a small pan, stir 125 ml (½ cup) water into the flour. Slowly add pan sauce. Cook on medium heat, while stirring, until thickened.
3. Season, to taste. Serve with pot roast.

"I love Canada's breathtaking wilderness. Hundreds of miles of raw beauty and wildlife."

"This meal reminds me of my Irish roots, it's a good way to remind us of our heritage. Sometimes my father threw in a little twist by making garlic mashed potatoes... Divine!"

FATHER'S BANGERS AND MASH

Peter Miller
Montreal, QC

Actor

SERVINGS 4 / PREPARATION 30 MIN / COOKING 30 MIN

INGREDIENTS

Sausages

8	lamb sausages
2	onions, sliced
2.5 ml (½ tsp)	dried mixed Italian herbs and fresh basil
5 ml (1 tsp)	mustard
625 ml (2 ½ cups)	vegetable broth
	Pink Himalayan salt, ground pepper
10 ml (2 tsp)	softened butter
10–20 ml (2–4 tsp)	plain flour

Mashed Patatoes

1 kg (2 lb)	potatoes, peeled, chopped
60 ml (¼ cup)	butter
	Milk, to taste

To Serve

625 ml (2 ½ cups)	fresh or frozen peas
	Fresh basil

PREPARATION

Preheat the oven to 200°C (400°F)

Sausages

1. Place the sausages into a roasting pan.
2. Put in the preheated oven and cook for 10 minutes. Turn the sausages and cook for another 5 minutes or until they have nice golden colour.
3. Add the onions to the pan.
4. Mix the dried herbs, mustard and broth together and pour over the sausages and onions.
5. Return the pan to the oven for a further 20 minutes, or until the sausages are cooked through and the onion gravy thickened. Season to taste, with salt and pepper.
6. Mix softened butter and plain flour together to form a paste.
7. Remove the sausages from the roasting pan, set aside and cover to keep warm.
8. Place the roasting pan onto the stove, add the flour and butter mix and whisk until combined to make a sauce. Stir over a medium-high heat 2–3 minutes or until the gravy has thickened slightly.
9. Add the sausages back to the pan and warm through 1–2 minutes. Set aside.

Mashed Patatoes

1. In a saucepan of boiling water, cook the potatoes until tender. Drain and mash.
2. Heat the butter and milk. Add a pinch of salt and pepper then pour over the mashed potatoes and mix until smooth. Set aside until ready to serve.

Peas

1. Cook the peas in a saucepan of boiling water if frozen 2–3 minutes or steam if fresh. Drain thoroughly and set aside.

To Serve

1. Serve the mash and peas with the onion gravy spooned over with sausages on the top. Add fresh basil to make the dish look nice.

 "My favourite thing to do is live in Montreal for the great restaurants. I love to socialize, eat and drink. My favourite place is called Brit & Chips in old Montreal! Great selection of draft beers and the best fish & chips in town. Canada is simply the best place to exist on this planet! I am very proud to be one of its sons."

"It is a staple in PEI, especially on Saturdays, to use up leftover salt cod from traditional Friday meals. Typically served with baked beans and green tomato chow or mustard pickles. This recipe builds on the traditional approach, with a modern zest."

FISH CAKES

The Honourable H. Wade MacLauchlan
West Covehead, PEI

Premier of Prince Edward Island

SERVINGS 20–24 / PREPARATION 1 H 30 MIN / COOKING 6–8 MIN

INGREDIENTS

8–10	medium-size wet variety, preferably older potatoes. Green Mountains, Red Chieftans, Fabula or any blue or yellow potatoes are great wet varieties.
250 ml (1 cup)	green, yellow or red onion, finely chopped
30 ml (2 tbsp)	fresh oregano or dill, finely chopped
454 g (1 lb)	fresh white fish, cod, haddock or halibut, depending on which is freshest and most readily available
454 g (1 lb)	salt cod (optional), can be fresh fish
4–5	limes or lemons, juiced
75—125 ml (⅓–½ cup)	cream cheese
2	eggs
	Pepper
	Nutmeg (optional)

Whatever the ingredients, there are three basic rules to successful fishcakes: they must be built, i.e., assembled in stages, they are better with as many fresh ingredients as possible and they are always better on the second or third day.

PREPARATION

Preheat oven to 160°C (325°F)

1. Boil the potatoes until firm to a fork, and remove from water to cool to room temperature. Shred and set aside.
2. Mix onions and fresh oregano. Set aside.
3. Rinse salt cod and rub off any salt. Soak salt cod at a medium heat for 1 hour or more, with at least one change of water.
4. Place the fresh fish in a platter and soak it with lime and/or lemon juice. Set the fish aside 20–25 minutes.
5. Drain the juice and place the fish in the oven at 160°C (325°F) 7–8 minutes, not too long, just till it's firm to the touch. Set the fish aside to cool. This method is more about curing the fish than cooking it.
6. Spread one quarter of the grated potatoes on the bottom of a large mixing bowl. Sprinkle one third of the onions-herbs mix over the potato, plus a generous grating of black pepper. If you like nutmeg, a light sprinkle of ground nutmeg will add a unique touch. Remember that a little nutmeg will go a long way. Don't overdo it.
7. Add one third of the fish. The white fish should come apart in flakes. The main thing is to handle it gently. The salt cod should be broken into small pieces and fragments.
8. Now for the secret touch: put dabs of cream cheese at regular intervals over the mixture.
9. Repeat the process, beginning with the potatoes. Go through the cycle twice. Finish with a layer of the final quarter of grated potatoes.
10. When the layering process has been completed, break two eggs over the mixture and fold the entire mixture together gently by hand. You'll know that you have done it well enough when your hands require a couple of good washings to get rid of the fishy smell.
11. The fish cakes will be better after they have a chance to marinate in the refrigerator for a few hours or even overnight, but you are not required to wait.
12. Use a cooking oil that can stand a reasonably high temperature, for example, peanut oil and ensure that the frying pan is hot before you put the fish cakes in. They should cook up to a nice brown crispness by frying 3–4 minutes on each side. Keep an eye on them to be sure they aren't sticking or burning.

"My favourite thing to see in Canada is the restoration of Province House in Prince Edward Island where the first meetings leading to Confederation took place in 1864."

"This recipe comes from my French Canadian mother Lucille."

FRENCH CANADIAN TOURTIERE

Alex Trebek
Sudbury, ON

Host of Jeopardy!

4 PIES / PREPARATION 2 H / COOKING 1 H

INGREDIENTS

Meat filling

1.5 kg (3 lb)	ground pork
1 kg (2 lb)	ground veal
4	large onions, finely chopped
45 ml (3 tbsp)	poultry seasoning
	Salt and pepper, to taste
1 package	poultry stuffing mix, dry

Crust

1.5 L (6 cups)	all-purpose flour
625 ml (2 ½ cups)	Crisco vegetable shortening
15 ml (1 tbsp)	salt
375 ml (1 ½ cups)	Ice water, approximately
	Milk

PREPARATION

Preheat oven 180°C (350°F)

Meat filling

1. In a large saucepan, combine the meat, onions and seasoning.
2. Add water to the top level of the meat.
3. Cook slowly for 1 hour.
4. Remove excess fat if any.
5. Add enough stuffing mix to absorb 90% of the liquid.
6. Allow to cool for 45 minutes.

Crust

1. In a large bowl, combine the flour and salt.
2. Stir the shortening into the flour using a pastry blender or two knives to get a grainy texture, where there are small pieces of shortening the size of peas.
3. Make a well in the center of mixture and pour the water in it.
4. Gently combine with a fork. Add some flour if pastry is too sticky.
5. Wrap the pastry in a plastic bag and let rest for at least 15 minutes before using.

Assembly

1. Roll out and line 4 foil pie plates with pastry.
2. Fill with the meat mixture.
3. Cover with a top crust; add holes.
4. Gently squeeze around edges.
5. Lightly brush the surface with milk.
6. Bake for 1 hour.

 "I love visiting the Byward Market in downtown Ottawa or just walking the streets of downtown Toronto. Both have given me great pleasure."

*"This recipe was passed down to my family by my grandmother.
It is of Ukranian origin. It's on the menu at my Toronto restaurant."*

GRANDMA GRETZKY'S GREAT PEROGIES

Wayne Gretzky
Brantford, ON

Former NHL Hockey Player

SERVINGS 24 / PREPARATION 45 MIN / COOKING 15 MIN

INGREDIENTS

Filling

2	large potatoes
1	onion, whole
5 ml (1 tsp)	butter
1	small onion, finely chopped
125 ml (½ cup)	cheddar cheese, grated
	Ground pepper

Pastry

250 ml (1 cup)	flour
1	egg yolk
1 dash	salt
60 ml (¼ cup)	boiling water

Cooking

2.5 ml (½ tsp)	salt
15 ml (1 tbsp)	oil

Finishing

15 ml (1 tbsp)	butter
2	green onions, chopped
	Sour cream, to taste
	Paprika, to taste

PREPARATION

Filling

1. Boil potatoes and whole onion until potatoes are fully cooked. Drain potatoes, discard onion and mash.
2. Sauté the chopped onions in butter until tender, but not browned.
3. Combine mashed potatoes, cheese and onion and mix well. Allow to cool.

Pastry

1. Combine all ingredients for pastry and mix together until mixture forms a ball.
2. Cover and let stand at room temperature for 30 minutes.
3. Roll dough to about 3 mm (⅛ in) thick.
4. Cut in circles of approximately 7 cm (3 in) diameter.
5. Place filling on half the circle, fold over and press edges together well, slightly dampening the edges with water to help seal, if necessary.
6. Fill a large saucepan ¾ full with water, add oil and salt for cooking and bring to a boil.
7. Add perogies and cook, uncovered, stirring occasionally with a wooden spoon to keep from sticking, for about 5 minutes (until they rise to the surface of the water).
8. Remove with slotted spoon.

Finishing

1. Saute in a frying pan with butter and chopped green onions for 2 minutes.
2. Garnish with sour cream and a dash of paprika.

"I travel a lot and coming back to my home in Brantford is always a great comfort."

"This dish reminds me of family reunions at my grandma's.
Getting this recipe on paper from grandma was a challenge."

GRANDMA'S MEATBALL STEW

Valérie Maltais
La Baie, QC

Olympic Medallist in Speed Skating

SERVINGS 8–10 / PREPARATION 45 MIN / COOKING 2 H

INGREDIENTS

1	whole chicken
1 kg (2 lb)	medium ground pork
2	onions, chopped
750 ml (3 cups)	homemade toasted flour or any other
	Salt and pepper
	Cold water
8	potatoes or more

" Sprinkle with ground cloves, cinnamon or nutmeg and serve with some pickled beets on the side. "

PREPARATION

1. Toast the flour in a cast iron skillet over low heat, stirring regularly until golden brown, or put the flour in a Pyrex dish and bake it at 200°C (400°F) until brown.
2. In a large pot, bring chicken, one onion, salt and pepper, to a boil, and simmer for 90 minutes.
3. Separate the chicken from the broth, debone the chicken and set broth and chicken aside separately in the refrigerator.
4. After 4 hours, remove the broth from the refrigerator and skim the congealed fat off surface of the broth.
5. Combine the ground pork, one minced onion, salt, pepper and spices.
6. Form small meatballs, roll them in white flour and add to chicken broth. Simmer for approximately 30 minutes.
7. Sift toasted flour into a bowl. Add some cold water and combine into a smooth paste.
8. Add this paste to broth using a sieve to avoid lumps. Thicken broth to desired consistency.
9. Add the chicken.
10. Boil potatoes and add to stew.
11. Serve with pickled beets.

"The Saguenay Fjord is an extraordinary place. My mother's house has an amazing view of the Fjord and every morning the first thing I do is go admire the view. It's very nice to go eat in a good restaurant and take a stroll down the seashore, especially when a cruise ship has docked."

"This recipe is from my native country, Haiti."

HAITIAN PORK GRIOT

Bruny Surin
Montreal, QC

Olympic Medallist in the 4 x 100 Metres Relay and Entrepreneur

SERVINGS 12 / PREPARATION 15 MIN / COOKING 1 H

INGREDIENTS

1.5 K (3 lb)	pork, fat removed, cubed
5 ml (1 tsp)	salt
1 medium	onion, sliced
5 ml (1 tsp)	instant chicken bouillon
5 ml (1 tsp)	wine vinegar
2	French shallots, quartered
2	garlic cloves, chopped
	Thyme and parsley herb bundle
	Chili pepper, to taste
2	limes, juiced
15 ml (1 tbsp)	cooking oil

PREPARATION

1. Rinse the meat in a bowl with tepid water; drain and pat dry.
2. Add salt, instant chicken bouillon, onion, vinegar, shallots and garlic; mix well.
3. Add lime juice, herb bundle and chili pepper; let marinate in the refrigerator for 60 minutes.
4. In a large saucepan, heat the oil and add the meat mixture. Be careful to keep the herb bundle and chili pepper on top.
5. Cover and let cook over low heat until the liquid is completely evaporated.
6. Remove from heat; let rest for a few minutes.
7. Brown meat in oil until golden on all sides.

"Montreal-based restaurant Bistrorante Boccone is one of my favourites. I love gathering there with my family and dear friends."

"Being from Charlevoix, I am still deeply attached to this region and I love to go back with my family and friends. The scenery is spectacular and the people are disarmingly generous. You can also find top-quality local products such as the Charlevoix lamb. From a basic recipe and inspired by many other lamb recipes, this particular one has evolved over the years. My wife Dorine incorporates fresh herbs we have on hand (never forgetting the rosemary) and, to add the crust that our children love, two of our family's favourites, Parmesan cheese and pistachios."

HERB-CRUSTED RACK OF LAMB

Martin Cauchon
La Malbaie, QC

President and CEO Groupe Capitales Medias

SERVINGS 4 / PREPARATION 15 MIN / COOKING 30 MIN

INGREDIENTS

Lamb

2	Quebec racks of lamb, about 675 g (1 ½ lb) each
45 ml (3 tbsp)	sunflower or olive oil
60 ml (4 tbsp)	Dijon mustard
	Salt and freshly ground pepper

Crust

2	cloves of garlic, minced
180 ml (¾ cup)	bread crumbs
30 ml (2 tbsp)	Parmesan cheese, finely grated
30 ml (2 tbsp)	rosemary, finely chopped
30 ml (2 tbsp)	fresh thyme, finely chopped
30 ml (2 tbsp)	parsley, finely chopped
30 ml (2 tbsp)	unsalted pistachios, crushed (optional)

PREPARATION

Preheat oven to 220°C (425°F)

1. Let the lamb rest at room temperature for about 20 minutes.
2. In the meantime prepare the crust: In a bowl, combine the garlic, bread crumbs, cheese, herbs and pistachios; set aside.
3. Season the lamb with salt and pepper.
4. Heat the oil over medium-high heat in a large frying pan and sear the lamb on each side, about 4 minutes per side. Remove the pan from the heat and wait a few minutes.
5. Brush the lamb racks, meat and bones, with Dijon mustard and coat with the crust mixture.
6. Place the lamb racks on a cooking dish and bake for about 15 minutes or until a meat thermometer inserted into the meat reads 50°C (120°F).
7. Remove from the oven and cover with aluminum foil for 5 minutes.
8. Cut the meat and serve with mashed potatoes and seasonal vegetables.

"My favourite place in Canada after Charlevoix, my dear native area, is Langara Island, British Columbia. Nature is breathtaking and the fishing exceptional."

"The Honey Bourbon barbecue recipe has not only become a family favourite, it is a huge hit at Ruby Watchco. The richness of bourbon combined with the sweetness of the honey creates a unique and rich flavor combination, not to mention the aroma. The recipe was developed as a way to utilize the incredible honey Chef Lora Kirk's bees have produced. This recipe is a perfect for summer time cooking as it is easy to prepare and will make you look like a culinary pro to your friends and family."

HONEY WHISKEY GLAZED CHICKEN

Lynn Crawford
Toronto, ON

Celebrity Chef

SERVINGS 4 / PREPARATION 10 MIN / COOKING 15–20 MIN

INGREDIENTS

Glaze

180 ml (¾ cup)	honey
15 ml (1 tbsp)	sriracha sauce
15 ml (1 tbsp)	whiskey
15 ml (1 tbsp)	Dijon mustard
	Zest of one orange
	Salt and pepper

Marinated Chicken

30 ml (2 tbsp)	olive oil
30 ml (2 tbsp)	whiskey
5 ml (1 tsp)	sriracha sauce
1	orange, juiced
2	thyme sprigs, leaves only
5 ml (1 tsp)	salt
1 ml (¼ tsp)	pepper
1	large clove garlic, grated
1	whole chicken about 1.5 kg (3 lb) backbone removed, cut into 8 pieces

PREPARATION

Glaze

1. In a small bowl, whisk together honey, sriracha sauce, whiskey, mustard and zest. Season to taste with salt and pepper, and set aside.

Marinated Chicken

1. In a large bowl, stir together oil, whiskey, sriracha sauce, orange juice, thyme, salt, pepper and garlic.
2. Add chicken and toss well to coat.
3. Refrigerate for 30 minutes.
4. Heat barbecue to medium, add chicken and grill until thoroughly cooked and no pink remains, 8–10 minutes per side.
5. Brush the chicken with glaze during the last 5 minutes of grilling time.

"Canada is an incredible country that embraces diversity, in fact celebrating our uniqueness is steeped into our culture and cuisine. It is because of this diversity that it is almost impossible for me to pick one favourite thing to do in Canada. Incredible things to do in Canada include salmon fishing in British Columbia, picking strawberries at the McLean Berry Farm in Ontario, preparing and eating the fresh, melt-in-your-mouth Fogo Island cod in Newfoundland. But if I have to pick one, my favourite place in Canada is my cottage in the Kawartha Lakes area of Ontario. There is nothing better than relaxing and hanging out at the lake with my friends and family."

"When I first moved to Toronto at the age of 19, my manager took me into her home while I was first starting out. Lentil dahl was (and is to this day) a regular staple in her house and has since become one of my favourite recipes to share amongst friends."

LENTIL DAHL

Serena Ryder
Millbrook, ON

Singer

SERVINGS 3–4 / PREPARATION 30 MIN / COOKING 15–20 MIN

INGREDIENTS

250 ml (1 cup)	red lentils, rinsed well
3 cm (1 in)	fresh ginger, sliced
2	bay leaves
30 ml (2 tbsp)	butter or ghee (preferably!)
1	large onion, finely chopped (don't cry)
2	garlic cloves, minced
10 ml (2 tsp)	ground turmeric
5 ml (1 tsp)	ground cumin
2.5 ml (½ tsp)	ground Garam Masala
2.5 ml (½ tsp)	chili flakes
30 ml (2 tbsp)	juice from the juiciest lemon you can find
2.5—5 ml (½–1 tsp)	sea salt, or just eyeball it
15 ml (1 tbsp)	cilantro leaves, chopped

PREPARATION

1. Place lentils, ginger, and bay leaves in a large saucepan with 750 ml (3 cups) of cold water. Bring to a boil, reduce the heat to medium and simmer, stirring to prevent sticking 10–12 minutes. Discard ginger and bay leaves, drain and set aside.

2. Heat the butter in a large frying pan over a medium-high heat. Add the onion and cook for 3 minutes. Stir in the garlic, turmeric, cumin, Garam Masala and chili flakes and cook for a further minute or until fragrant. Stir in the lemon juice and season to taste with salt.

3. Add the lentils to the pan and mix well. Cook for a further 3 minutes, stirring constantly.

4. Remove from heat.

5. Stir in cilantro leaves and serve hot over basmati rice.

"When I'm at home in Toronto, I love to go to the Art Gallery of Ontario. It's so inspiring and such a beautiful space to just clear my head and fill my cup."

"With Italian roots, this recipe is a family tradition in Nova Scotia.
It's the perfect first date recipe, as it requires you to dig in with your hands and get a little messy!"

LOBSTER FRA DIAVOLO

The Honourable Sandy Silver
Dawson City, YT

Premier of Yukon

SERVINGS 4 / PREPARATION 30 MIN / COOKING 45 MIN

INGREDIENTS

Marinara Sauce

90 ml (6 tbsp)	olive oil
60 ml (¼ cup)	butter
3	garlic cloves, mashed
16	fresh parsley leaves, chopped
3 ml (½ tsp)	black pepper
3 ml (½ tsp)	salt
1.5 L (6 cups)	tomatoes, diced (canned)
15 ml (1 tbsp)	dried oregano
8	anchovy fillets chopped, or guts from ½ the lobsters used in Fra Diavolo
30 ml (2 tbsp)	tomato paste

Lobster

4	lobsters 700 g—900 g (1 ½–2 lb each)
8	fresh sprigs parsley leaves, chopped
1	garlic clove, mashed
125 ml (½ cup)	butter
60 ml (¼ cup)	olive oil
340 g (¾ lb)	onions, diced
1 pinch	salt
1 ml (¼ tsp)	crushed red pepper
2 ml (⅓ tsp)	freshly ground black pepper
1 L (4 cups)	warm marinara sauce
454 g (1 lb)	spaghetti

PREPARATION

Marinara sauce

1. Sauté garlic and parsley in butter and oil slowly for 2 minutes.
2. Add salt and pepper. Add tomatoes and oregano; cook slowly for 20 minutes.
3. Add anchovies and tomato paste, stir well, and remove from heat.

Lobster

1. Split live lobsters lengthwise down the middle.
2. Remove head sacs and intestinal veins; and discard these.
3. Combine butter and olive oil in a large skillet and heat.
4. Add onions and sauté slowly to medium brown; it is very important for the flavour to make sure they begin to caramelize.
5. Add lobsters, meat side down, and sauté for 5 minutes.
6. Turn lobsters, add parsley and garlic and stir well. Cook for 5 minutes.
7. Add salt, red and black pepper, and marinara sauce.
8. Stir, cover and cook for 10 minutes.
9. Uncover and cook for 10 minutes.
10. Serve over cooked spaghetti.
11. Lobster can be cooled and refrigerated or frozen at step 8.

" *If refrigerated, heat on medium–low heat and heat through (do not re-boil).*

If frozen, defrost at room temperature for a few hours or over a day or so in the fridge, then reheat well (do not re-boil). Add tomato paste to thicken if needed. "

"I always look forward to enjoying the Dawson City Music Festival. This dynamic festival transcends our community, bringing everyone together. I've volunteered for many years and it's one of the best parts of my summer."

"This is from my grandmother. A recipe from her Portuguese roots."

MARIA ALICE'S STUFFED SQUID

Keshia Chanté
Ottawa, ON

Singer

SERVINGS 5 / PREPARATION 20 MIN / COOKING 40–45 MIN

INGREDIENTS

Squid

5	large squids or smaller ones but they are a little harder to stuff

Stuffing

454 g (1 lb)	ground beef
1–2	Chouriço (Portugese pork sausage), to taste, chopped
1	large onion, chopped
1	garlic clove, minced
5 ml (1 tsp)	thyme
5 ml (1 tsp)	italian seasoning
1	bay leaf
15 ml (1 tbsp)	flour
	Salt and Pepper

Broth

1	large onion, chopped
1	tomato, diced
2	potatoes, cubed
1	garlic clove, minced
5 ml (1 tsp)	thyme
1	bay leaf
500 ml (2 cups)	white wine
	Salt and pepper

PREPARATION

Squid

1. Clean the squids and make sure you remove the inside without breaking the bags. Chop the tentacles off and set aside.

Stuffing

1. In a large skillet sauté, the onion, garlic, salt, pepper, thyme, Italian spices, chouriço, bay leaf, until all ingredients look blended.
2. Add ground beef and tentacles from the squid, stir until meat is cooked.
3. Add flour to help keep the meat and spices together, acting almost like a glue.
4. Let cool.
5. Stuff the squids but do not overstuff. Apply a solid toothpick to the end so it does not open.

Broth

1. In a large saucepan, add onion, tomato, garlic, salt, pepper, thyme, bay leaf, white wine, and stir until onions become translucent. Then add potatoes, if you want, and cook them for about 10 minutes.
2. At this time, add the squid, lower the heat and cover.
3. Let cook 20–25 minutes, stirring sparingly.

"My best thing to do in Canada is visit Muskoka and enjoy the beautiful cottage country."

"My family makes fun of me because they think I can't cook, but honestly this is the best meatloaf ever.
I used to make this with my kids when they were little but it's been ages, so,
recently I decided to make it with my grandkids, Wyatt and Emily. Boy, did we have fun!
I loved the fact that I'm sharing this with the next generation and I think they loved it too!"

MIKE HOLMES'S
FAMOUS HUMONGOUS MEATLOAF

Mike Holmes
Halton Hills, ON

TV Show Host, HGTV Canada

SERVINGS 10–12 / PREPARATION 30 MIN / COOKING 1 H 30 MIN

INGREDIENTS

Meatloaf

2	eggs, beaten
250 ml (1 cup)	cottage cheese
1—1.225 kg (2–2 ½ lb)	ground sirloin (I like a lot of meat!)
125 ml (½ cup)	onions, finely chopped
1 box	Stove Top cornbread stuffing
125 ml (½ cup)	ketchup
170 ml (⅔ cup)	sweet and sour sauce
	Sea salt
4–5	thick slices of Black Forest ham
500 ml (2 cups)	grated 3-cheese mix for center of meatloaf

Finishing

15 ml (1 tbsp)	butter
125 ml (½ cup)	onions, finely chopped
250 ml (1 cup)	water
250 ml (1 cup)	grated 3-cheese mix for topping
170 ml (⅔ cup)	sweet and sour sauce
60 ml (¼ cup)	ketchup
A couple shakes	Frank's Red Hot Sauce, to taste

" *I go to my local butcher and get ground sirloin and thickly sliced Black Forest ham.* "

PREPARATION

Preheat oven: Standard to 190°C (375°F)/Convection to 180°C (350°F)

Meatloaf

1. Beat eggs; mix in cottage cheese and set aside.
2. Mix ground meat, half of the chopped onions, ketchup and half of the sweet and sour sauce.
3. Add eggs and cottage cheese to meat mixture until nicely mixed.
4. Pack down into a thick pancake.
5. Place slices of Black Forest ham in center, add 500 ml (2 cups) of grated 3-cheese mix and roll into a tube.
6. Form meat mixture around the ham so it looks like a loaf of crusty bread.
7. Make a reservoir down the middle and fill with cheese.
   Yes, I like a lot of cheese!

Finishing

1. Place meatloaf in a buttered oval roasting pan. Add onions and about 2.5 cm (1 in) of water around the meatloaf. About 250 ml (1 cup).
2. Top with grated 3-cheese mix.
3. Drizzle sweet and sour sauce, ketchup and hot sauce on top; cover with lid or aluminum foil.
4. Cook for 90 minutes or until cooked thoroughly. At 45 minutes, take the lid off and allow top to brown. Baste at the hour mark; put under the broiler for the last 15 minutes.
5. Once cooked, remove from the oven and let it rest for at least 10 minutes.
6. Then slice and spoon juice over the meatloaf—the juice is the best part!
7. Serve with mashed potatoes and green beans or whatever sides you like.

"My favourite place to be during the summer months is on my boat on Lake Ontario—it's my true happy place. It's where can really relax and decompress. When I can't be on my boat I'm incredibly lucky to have the Niagara Escarpment as my backyard. Spending time walking my dog, Charlie, and listening to the sound of nature is so amazingly peaceful.

In the fall and winter, I love being outside—jumping on my ATV or Skidoo is a great way to enjoy the outdoors. We are lucky to live in an area that offers so many options, like Grey and Bruce Counties."

"This is my Mom's recipe, and I grew up with this."

MINI TURKEY LOAVES

Elizabeth Manley
Ottawa, ON

Olympic Medallist in Figure Skating

Credit: Valerie Keeler

SERVINGS 6–8 / PREPARATION 15 MIN / COOKING 40 MIN

INGREDIENTS

Turkey loaves

10 ml (2 tsp)	vegetable oil
1	medium onion, chopped
½	large green pepper
2	large eggs
125 ml (½ cup)	Italian-style bread crumbs
125 ml (½ cup)	milk
45 ml (3 tbsp)	steak sauce or barbecue sauce
15 ml (1 tbsp)	Dijon mustard
3 ml (¾ tsp)	salt
2 ml (½ tsp)	pepper
1 kg (2 lb)	ground lean turkey

Glaze

75 ml (⅓ cup)	chili sauce or ketchup
15 ml (1 tbsp)	brown sugar
5 ml (1 tsp)	cider vinegar

PREPARATION

Preheat oven to 180°C (350°F)

1. Line a baking sheet with foil.
2. In a medium skillet, heat oil, add onions and peppers and cook until softened. About 8 minutes.
3. Transfer to a large bowl and let cool about 10 minutes.
4. Add eggs, bread crumbs, milk, steak sauce, mustard, salt and pepper to the cooled onion and pepper mixture. Stir to combine.
5. Add ground turkey. By hand or with a large spatula, mix until all ingredients are thoroughly combined.
6. Divide turkey mixture into 6–8 equal portions. Shape into ovals and place on a prepared baking sheet.
7. Bake for 30 minutes.

Glaze

1. In a small bowl, combine chili sauce, brown sugar and vinegar. Mix well.
2. Spoon glaze onto loaves and return to the oven. Continue baking until loaves are heated through or when the temperature reaches 180ºC (350ºF), about 8 minutes.
3. Let loaves stand 10 minutes and serve.

"Having had the amazing opportunity to travel across Canada, there are so many incredible places to visit. From experiencing the fantastic Canada Day Celebrations in the nation's capital, to the beautiful ferry rides in majestic British Columbia, and eating the best lobster you can imagine in the Maritimes. Happy Birthday, Canada!"

"Madame Murphy is my grandmother, Yvette. Every summer, she prepared this stew with vegetables from her garden. We loved eating it with a slice of house bread and a few splashes of vinegar. To me, this recipe is typical of the great big French-Canadian families."

MADAME MURPHY'S STEW

Véronic DiCaire
Embrun, ON

Credit: Julien Cauvin

Impersonator and Singer

SERVINGS 4 / PREPARATION 40 MIN / COOKING 3–4 H

INGREDIENTS

1 kg (2 lb)	beef chuck or bone-in sirloin roast, cubed 4 cm (1 ½ in)
1	large onion, sliced
2–3	slices 5 mm (¼ in) thick of salted lard, diced. Do not use bacon as a substitute!
	Pepper
6	whole carrots or the same amount in small garden carrots
	Green and yellow beans, to taste
8–10	baby potatoes
1	turnip, cut into pieces
1	cabbage, quartered

PREPARATION

1. In a Creuset French Oven, add meat, onion, lard, pepper and cover with water 4 cm (1 ½ in) above the meat.
2. Bring to a boil 15–20 minutes while removing the foam.
3. Cover and cook on low heat until meat is very tender, 3-4 hours.
4. Add carrots, beans, potatoes, turnip and cabbage. Make sure the liquid covers at least half the meat.
5. Cover again to finish cooking, until vegetables are done.

❝ *Bon appétit!* **❞**

 "My favourite place in Canada is Ottawa's Rideau Canal, for its skating rink and hot chocolate during winter and for the kindness of the people of my native area."

"This is a secret recipe from the road."

MOOSE MEAT MARINADE

Ron James
Toronto, ON

Actor and Comedian

SERVINGS 6–8 / PREPARATION 15 MIN / COOKING 1 H 30 MIN – 2 H

INGREDIENTS

2—3 kg (4–6 lb)	moose meat or moose neck roast
250 ml (1 cup)	red wine
2	cooking onions, chopped
5	garlic cloves, minced
15 ml (1 tbsp)	Worcestershire sauce
75 ml (⅓ cup)	olive oil
15 ml (1 tbsp)	Dijon mustard
5	whole juniper berries
4 ml (¼ tbsp)	salt
5 ml (1 tsp)	fresh ground pepper
8 ml (½ tbsp)	thyme
8 ml (½ tbsp)	rosemary
8 ml (½ tbsp)	oregano

PREPARATION

1. Mix all ingredients together in a pot or plastic food bag.
2. Add meat to the marinade and massage it until the roast is smothered on both sides.
3. Allow the meat to marinate 12–24 hours in the fridge.
4. Remove from the marinade and pat dry.
5. Heat a skillet, add some oil and sear the moose meat on all sides until golden.
6. Slowly cook the meat, covered, on the barbecue at 100°C (200°F) or in the oven, until the meat has an internal temperature of 60°C (140°F) or until it's easily shredded.
7. Serve with assorted morel mushrooms, carrots and baby potatoes.

"I absolutely love to hike Gros Morne National Park as well as the Selkirk Mountains in B.C. Nothing beats swimming in the Atlantic Ocean in August and drinking Dark and Stormy cocktails with old friends."

"I went to Morocco a few years ago and had tagine chicken every night. I also saw a wingless owl fight a snake. Interesting place."

MOROCCAN CHICKEN TAGINE WITH SQUASH

Darrin Rose
Oshawa, ON

Actor and Comedian

SERVINGS 2 / PREPARATION 10 MIN / COOKING 25 MIN

INGREDIENTS

2	chicken breasts, cubed
1	garlic clove
15 ml (1 tbsp)	butter
250 ml (1 cup)	chicken broth
15 ml (1 tbsp)	ground cinnamon
8 ml (½ tbsp)	ground ginger
2	lemons
250 ml (1 cup)	Castelvetrano olives
250 ml (1 cup)	butternut or summer squash, cubed
1 pinch	saffron
	Cooked couscous (enough for at least two servings)

PREPARATION

1. In a skillet on medium heat, melt butter and garlic together.
2. Add chicken and brown it on all sides; remove the chicken/garlic from the skillet.
3. Turn the burner down to low heat. Add broth, cinnamon and ginger; stir well.
4. Squeeze all juice from one lemon into the broth.
5. Add chicken and garlic to the broth, along with the olives and squash; stir.
6. Cut the second lemon into circular slices. Put 4–5 slices on top of the mixture in the skillet; add a large pinch of saffron.
7. Cover and let simmer on low heat 15–20 minutes.
8. Serve over couscous. Spoon some of the broth onto the couscous.

♡ *"I love the Ogopogo statue in Kelowna, a tribute to the legendary sea monster that haunts Okanagan Lake. I respect the aplomb of a people who created a legend out of what was, in all likelihood, a floating log."*

"The three main ingredients, salmon, maple syrup and fiddleheads are local New Brunswick favourites.
The recipe is full of flavour while also being incredibly healthy.
It has quickly become a favourite for Karine and me."

NEW BRUNSWICK CEDAR PLANK MAPLE SALMON AND FIDDLEHEAD SAUTÉ

**The Honourable
Brian Gallant**
Shediac, NB

Premier of New Brunswick

SERVINGS 4–6 / PREPARATION 5 MIN / COOKING 8–10 MIN

INGREDIENTS

Maple Salmon

1 kg (2 lb)	salmon fillet
45 ml (3 tbsp)	vegetable oil
23 ml (1 ½ tbsp)	soy sauce
8 ml (1 ½ tsp)	garlic, chopped
3 ml (½ tsp)	salt
1 ml (¼ tsp)	white pepper
80 ml (⅓ cup)	rye or Scotch whiskey
15 ml (1 tbsp)	maple syrup

Fiddlehead Sauté

454 g (1 lb)	fiddleheads, cleaned
60 ml (¼ cup)	butter
125 ml (½ cup)	onion, finely minced
15 ml (1 tbsp)	garlic, minced
15 ml (1 tbsp)	lemon juice
15 ml (1 tbsp)	maple syrup
5 ml (1 tsp)	paprika
	Salt and pepper, to taste

PREPARATION

Preheat oven to 200°C (400°F)

1. Prepare two large saucepans of boiling salted water. Dip fiddleheads into a first saucepan and blanch for 1 minute; drain and discard water. Repeat in the second pan, then immerse in ice water to stop cooking. Drain and set aside.

2. Place salmon fillets in a long shallow dish.

3. In a bowl, mix all ingredients and pour over salmon fillets. Marinate for 30 minutes.

4. Place cedar plank directly on the oven rack and bake 8–10 minutes. This will lightly toast the wood.

5. In the meantime, in a stainless steel frying pan, heat butter over medium-high heat. Fry onion and garlic for 2 minutes. Add fiddleheads and stir well; sprinkle with salt, pepper, lemon juice, maple syrup and paprika while stirring constantly. Sauté until fiddleheads are tender, 3–5 minutes. Set aside.

6. Remove the plank from the oven and rub with a thin coating of olive oil while plank is still hot. Place salmon directly on the hot plank and roast on the plank for about 10 minutes.

" *Enjoy immediately!* **"**

"New Brunswick is home to some of the most breathtaking natural treasures in the world, which is why we often choose to explore places close to home, such as Hopewell Rocks." – Brian Gallant

"This recipe comes from Chef Colin Griffin who works at my restaurant, Le Rosewood, in Old Montreal."

OLIVE OIL POACHED COD & SIDES

Jonas Tomalty
Montreal, QC

Singer and Entrepreneur

SERVING 1 / PREPARATION 40 MIN / COOKING 20 MIN

INGREDIENTS

Cod

150 g (⅓ lb)	cod pavé, skinned
20 ml (4 tsp)	olive oil
1.25 ml (¼ tsp)	lavender
2.5 ml (½ tsp)	lemon zest
2.5 ml (½ tsp)	rosemary, finely chopped
1 small pinch	juniper, fresh, ground
1 very small pinch	salt

Pea Puree

340 g (¾ lb)	green peas, fresh
750 ml (3 cups)	light fish stock (fumet)
60 ml (¼ cup)	olive oil
	Salt

Light Remoulade Sauce

150 ml (⅔ cup)	mayonnaise
60 ml (¼ cup)	buttermilk
25 ml (⅛ cup)	Dijon mustard
30 ml (2 tbsp)	white wine vinegar
15 ml (1 tbsp)	capers, chopped
2	scallions, green part only, chopped
	Salt and pepper

Apple Cider Vinegar Dressing

2 L (8 cups)	apple cider, fresh pressed
200 ml (⅘ cup)	apple cider vinegar
1	thyme branch
12	peppercorns
200 ml (⅘ cup)	olive oil
	Salt

Veggies

115 g (¼ lb)	mixed summer vegetables (sliced fingerling potatoes, zucchini, celeriac, radish and fennel)
1	apple, diced
1 pinch	chives
50 g (1.7 oz)	lump, knuckle or leg crab meat pieces, chopped coarsely (pick out bits of shell)

Salad

A variety of picked herbs (fennel fronds, carrot tops 2.5 cm (1 in), cut chives, parsley leaves, tarragon leaves, red sorrel and mint all work well)

25 ml (⅛ cup)	apple cider vinegar dressing
1 small pinch	salt

PREPARATION

Cod

1. Place all cod ingredients in a vacuum sealer bag; seal lightly
2. Poach vacuum sealed cod in simmering water, about 8 minutes, or until done. Let rest in bag in a warm spot.

Pea Puree

1. Poach peas in fumet until just barely cooked. Strain, reserving the fumet.
2. Place peas in a blender with 125 ml (½ cup) fumet and 60 ml (¼ cup) olive oil.
3. Puree and add more fumet progressively until the desired consistency is achieved.
4. Season, set aside the remaining fumet.

Light Remoulade Sauce

1. Place all in cup, and using a hand blender, puree until smooth.
2. Thin with 60 ml (¼ cup) apple cider vinegar dressing. Set aside.

Apple Cider Vinegar Dressing

1. Simmer apple cider to reduce to 625 ml (2 ½ cups), strain into a bowl.
2. Stir in apple cider vinegar and let cool.
3. Whisk in olive oil, season, set aside.

Veggies

1. Combine barely warm mixed summer vegetables with diced apple, a pinch of chives and 60 ml (¼ cup) light remoulade sauce.
2. Fold in 50 g (1.7 oz) of lump, knuckle or leg crab meat pieces. Taste, season and keep warm.

Salad

1. In a small bowl, toss picked herbs with 25 ml (⅛ cup) apple cider vinegar dressing and a small pinch of salt. Set aside.

Assembly

1. Heat 75 ml (⅓ cup) green pea puree, using a small amount of reserved light fish fumet, if required. Check seasoning, keep warm.
2. On a large plate spread the pea puree. Open the vacuum sealer bag containing the cod, gently pat it dry, sprinkle with a little fresh-cut parsley or chives and place the cod on the puree.
3. In little bits, place the crab salad around the periphery, irregularly.
4. Place half of the herb salad on the cod, don't hide the fish and place the remainder around the plate, irregularly, to complete the dish.
5. Add a few drips of olive oil.

"I love owning a restaurant in this beautiful city called home. Old Montreal has a lot of history, a great place to be!"

"This is my wife Pascale Vallée's recipe."

PEACH SALMON

Rodger Brulotte
Montreal, QC

Baseball Analyst

SERVINGS 2 / PREPARATION 15 MIN / COOKING 20 MIN

INGREDIENTS

1	salmon fillet, skin removed 680 g (1.5 lb)
796 ml (28 oz)	peach (canned) [keep 30 ml (2 tbsp) of the juice]
45 ml (3 tbsp)	honey
8 ml (1 ½ tsp)	tamari sauce
8 ml (1 ½ tsp)	sesame seeds
	Fresh ground salt and pepper

PREPARATION

Preheat the oven to 180°C (350°F)

1. Slice peaches lengthwise and place them in a rectangular glass or ceramic baking dish such as Pyrex. Add peach juice.
2. Rinse the salmon and pat it dry with paper towel; place in the dish.
3. Add honey on top of the salmon; add tamari sauce and sprinkle with sesame seeds.
4. Add salt and pepper, to taste.
5. Cover with tin foil and bake in the oven for about 20 minutes, depending on the thickness of the salmon or until cooked according to taste.
6. Serve with baby potatoes and green salad.

" *Your guests will ask for more!* **"**

"I very much like Le Mirage Golf Club in Terrebonne, Quebec."

"My mother's family settled in Montreal coming from the Abruzzo region in Italy in 1915. Great food has always been an important part of our family life, especially with my grandfather Albino Arsenio Cappelli. He adored good food and passed down to me the family version of this Abruzzi poached fish pasta. The cinnamon is a Quebecois addition, taken from a well-known pizzeria in the neighbourhood that added cinnamon to their tomato sauce. The garlic diffuses in the sauce so don't let the amount scare you! We obviously love garlic!"

Sean Power
Toronto, ON

Actor

PESCI DI CAPPELLI
(POACHED FISH PASTA)

SERVINGS 7–8 / PREPARATION 20 MIN / COOKING 15 MIN

INGREDIENTS

30 ml (2 tbsp)	olive oil
3–4	large carrots, thinly sliced
1	bulb of garlic, chopped roughly
1 big pinch	sea salt
2	cans of organic tomatoes
6	anchovy fillets
375 ml (1 ½ cups)	water
250 ml (1 cup)	white wine
15 ml (1 tbsp)	cinnamon
3	salmon or cod fillets
	Extra virgin olive oil
500 g (17.6 oz) (2 packages)	pasta (linguini or tagliatelle), cooked in salted water
	Parmesan cheese

PREPARATION

1. In a deep frying pan and over medium-high heat, add the olive oil, carrots, garlic and salt. Fry until the mixture starts to yellow, do not brown the garlic.
2. Add tomatoes, anchovies, water, wine and cinnamon. There should be enough liquid so the mixture looks like soup. It will reduce. Add salt, to taste and simmer uncovered until the carrots are soft.
3. Add fish making sure to cover with the sauce, and poach for about 7 minutes. If too reduced, add more wine.
4. Halve the fillets and check that they are cooked through.
5. Take off heat, stir in a few tablespoons of quality extra virgin olive oil.
6. Serve with pasta and Parmesan cheese.

❝ *Buon appetito!* **❞**

 "Montreal is my favourite place in Canada. From an early idyllic childhood on Île-des-Sœurs, to living on the Plateau and attending Ecole Nationale de Théâtre du Canada, I love everything about Montreal. The warm summers, the snowy winters, the beautiful women. I love plays by Michel Tremblay, St-Laurent smoked meat and late night St-Viateur bagels. Montreal's arts culture promotes the people and the people promote the arts culture which creates a sustained ideal of what it means to be Québécois. J'aime Montréal!"

"This recipe was inspired by my mother-in-law's family, who are Appalachians natives. When I prepare it, my house is filled with such an amazing aroma, which comforts me during the coldest months."

PORK AND BEEF ROAST

Marie-Christine Depestre
Montreal, QC

Singer

SERVINGS 16 / PREPARATION 30 MIN / COOKING 4 H

INGREDIENTS

1 kg (2 lb)	beef chuck roast with bone
1 kg (2 lb)	pork roast
4	carrots, cut into sections
1	large turnip, cubed
4 medium	potatoes, cubed
1	large onion, cut into 12 pieces
4	garlic cloves
500 ml (2 cups)	veal stock
1 L (4 cups)	beef broth
30 ml (2 tbsp)	half-salt butter
	Salt and pepper

PREPARATION

Preheat the oven to 160°C (325°F)

1. In a large skillet, sear the beef and pork on all sides in butter. Add some olive oil if necessary.
2. Season with salt and pepper; place in a large roasting pan.
3. Insert 2 cloves of garlic deeply into each piece of meat.
4. Add all vegetables.
5. Add broth and stock; adjust seasoning.
6. Cover and bake in the oven for at least 4 hours or until the meat comes off easily with a fork.

❝ *Enjoy!* ❞

 "The Atwater market in Montreal is a must for me. I love spending a whole afternoon shopping, having a little bite to eat and walking along the Lachine Canal. Lots of fun!"

*"My partner and I ate this tartar in the Gaspé Peninsula, Quebec, during a road trip.
As we often do, we had fun detecting the ingredients found in the dish. Then we replicated it at home,
adding and removing ingredients. We adapted it our way!"*

QUEBEC CIDER SALMON TARTAR

Ingrid Falaise
Montreal, QC

Actress, Author and Speaker

Credit: Andréanne Gauthier

SERVING 1 / PREPARATION 10 MIN

INGREDIENTS

Tartar

150 g (⅓ lb)	salmon, chopped
15 ml (1 tbsp)	green apple, finely diced
5 ml (1 tsp)	shallots, chopped
20 ml (4 tsp)	Quebec cider, reduced to one quarter or 5 ml (1 tsp)
10 ml (2 tsp)	white balsamic vinegar
15 ml (1 tbsp)	cilantro, chopped
5 ml (1 tsp)	fresh ginger, finely chopped
1.25 ml (¼ tsp)	Sambal Oelek chili paste
5 ml (1 tsp)	olive oil
5 ml (1 tsp)	mango and pineapple chutney

Garnish

10 ml (2 tsp)	red tobiko (fish roe)
4	fine apple slices
	Salt and pepper
	Half a baguette

PREPARATION

1. In a large bowl, add all tartar ingredients; mix well. Season, to taste.
2. Arrange the tartar in a round cookie cutter on a large plate.
3. Place apple slices on top of the tartar in the shape of a fan.
4. Add tobiko on top.
5. Finely slice the baguette and place the slices on a baking tray. Brush with olive oil. Add salt and pepper.
6. Brown in the oven until crisp.
7. Serve with tartar.

 "As we love sports and the outdoors, we spend our winters hurtling down mountains and our summers sailing on lakes. Skiing in winter, on a board during summer, a fishing rod in my hand or snowshoes on my feet, I love Quebec for its beautiful nature, fauna and flora!"

"This is one of the first adult dishes I learned to make on my own when I wasn't travelling on tour across Canada. It's a family recipe that has several variations but feels like home to me when I make it."

QUINOA WITH STUFFED CHICKEN AND ASPARAGUS

Tyler Shaw
Coquitlam, BC

Singer

Credit: Mathew Guido

SERVINGS 2 / PREPARATION 15 MIN / COOKING 45 MIN

INGREDIENTS

2	chicken breasts
	Olive oil
	Salt and pepper, to taste
10 ml (2 tsp)	grape seed oil
250 ml (1 cup)	spinach
250 ml (1 cup)	mozzarella cheese, grated
15 ml (1 tbsp)	butter
2	garlic cloves, minced
500 ml (2 cups)	asparagus
125 ml (½ cup)	quinoa
250 ml (1 cup)	chicken broth

PREPARATION

Preheat oven to 180°C (350°F)

Chicken

1. Carefully butterfly both of the raw chicken breasts.
2. Rub with olive oil and lightly dust with salt and pepper.
3. Heat your grape seed oil in a pan on medium–high heat.
4. Place chicken into the pan and sear on both sides.
5. Place chicken into a casserole dish.
6. Place spinach and mozzarella cheese inside the chicken.
7. Place chicken inside oven 15–20 minutes or until cooked.

Asparagus

1. Melt butter in pan. Toss garlic in 1–2 minutes.
2. Toss asparagus into the pan. Stir occasionally 7–10 minutes.

Quinoa

1. Place 125 ml (½ cup) of quinoa in a pot. Add chicken broth.
2. Bring to a boil, reduce heat and let simmer covered 15–20 minutes.
3. Remove from heat and let sit for 5 minutes.

"Canada is my home. My father is from Hong Kong and my mother is of Polish and Eastern European descent. I was raised with the understanding that food is one of the key ingredients in the recipe of family. I am very fortunate to have an opportunity to experience various cultures through food, here in Canada."

159

"This is a personal creation."

RAVETTO AI FUNGHI
(CELERIAC RISOTTO WITH MUSHROOMS)

Yves Desjardins-Siciliano
Montreal, QC

President and Chief Executive Officer,
VIA Rail Canada Inc.

SERVINGS 2 / PREPARATION 20 MIN / COOKING 30 MIN

INGREDIENTS

1 L (4 cups)	chicken broth
30 ml (2 tbsp)	olive oil
	Unsalted butter
3	French shallots, peeled, finely chopped
2	cloves of garlic, peeled, finely chopped
500 ml (2 cups)	celeriac/celery root, sliced on mandolin, then very finely chopped to rice-size shape
200 ml (⅘ cup)	dry white wine
250 ml (1 cup)	wild mushrooms, wiped clean, chopped
5	sprigs of thyme, leaves picked
190 ml (¾ cup)	flat-leaf parsley, very finely chopped
250 g (1 cup)	freshly grated Parmigiano-Reggiano cheese plus a bit extra for grating over at service

PREPARATION

1. On medium heat, add 15 ml (1 tbsp) of olive oil in frying pan. Fry the mushrooms until they are cooked through, and season with salt and pepper. Add garlic, thyme, parsley and butter and mix together; set aside.
2. In a medium saucepan, heat the broth.
3. In a separate pan, add 15 ml (1 tbsp) of olive oil and a knob of butter, add the shallots and the garlic, cook slowly without letting it colour.
4. When softened, add the celeriac and turn up the heat.
5. Keep stirring the celeriac as it lightly fries.
6. Add wine when celeriac looks slightly translucent and glossy; keep stirring.
7. Once the wine has cooked into the celeriac, add a ladle of hot broth and a good pinch of salt. Turn the heat down to a simmer and keep adding a ladleful of broth at a time, stirring and massaging, allowing liquid to be absorbed before you add another. This will take about 15 minutes but you will need to taste test to check doneness. Keep adding broth until the celeriac is soft but still has a little bite. If you run out of broth just use some boiled water.
8. Stir in cooked mushrooms and Parmesan cheese.
9. Serve with grated Parmesan cheese, to taste.

" Voilà! A healthy alternative to traditional risotto. "

"Canadian maple syrup goes with anything, anytime. At breakfast on Greek yogurt with Saskatoon or Lac St-Jean berries, at lunch in a dressing over a Brome Lake duck salad with pine nuts and soft Quebec goat cheese, or at dinner over smoked ham. For me, it's a sweet, authentic and uniquely Canadian flavour."

"Growing up in rural B.C., I was raised on organic food from my grandfather's farm and what we hunted from the wild. Canadian moose was a staple in my family and I ate it from an early age. I was about 17 years old when I came up with this recipe."

RICK'S MOOSE CHILI

Rick Hansen
Richmond, BC

Former Paralympian Medallist and
Founder & CEO, Rick Hansen Foundation

SERVINGS 8–10 / PREPARATION 15 MIN / COOKING 1 H 30 MIN – 2 H

INGREDIENTS

30 ml (2 tbsp)	vegetable oil
540 ml (19 oz)	kidney beans (canned)
454 g (1 lb)	moose, substitute lean ground beef or without meat
1	large onion, chopped
1	large green, red or orange bell pepper, chopped
1	large celery stalk, chopped
1	garlic clove, minced or 3 ml (½ tsp) of garlic powder
5 ml (1 tsp)	paprika
1 ml (¼ tsp)	cayenne pepper
5 ml (1 tsp)	salt
15—23 ml (1–1 ½ tbsp)	chili powder, to taste
796 ml (28 oz)	stewed tomatoes, chopped (canned)
568—852 ml (20–30 oz)	whole mushrooms (canned)
398 ml (14 oz)	tomato sauce
1	bay leaf
156 ml (5.5 oz)	tomato paste

PREPARATION

1. In a small saucepan, add some oil and sauté the moose until browned.
2. Add onion, garlic and chopped vegetables stirring often; cook for 5 minutes.
3. Add beans, tomatoes, tomato sauce and mushrooms.
4. Add spices, bay leaf and allow to simmer for as long as possible. I let mine simmer 4–6 hours.
5. Remove bay leaf before serving.

❝ *This chili freezes well.* ❞

*"Atlin Lake is the largest natural lake in B.C. and one of the most beautiful places in Canada.
I enjoy visiting with friends there and touring the historic gold mine and town. And of course, I love the fishing!"*

"The recipe is from my mother Helen, handed down to her from her mother who was a Greek immigrant in Brooklyn, New York."

ROASTED LEG OF LAMB STUFFED WITH GARLIC

Bret Hart
Calgary, AB

Former Professional Wrestler

SERVINGS 6–8 / PREPARATION 10 MIN / COOKING 2–2 H 30 MIN

INGREDIENTS

3 kg (6–7 lb)	bone-in leg of lamb, trimmed of excess fat
5–6	cloves of garlic, cut into long slivers
125 ml (½ cup)	white vinegar
	Sea salt
	Fresh cracked ground pepper

PREPARATION

Preheat oven to 160°C (325°F)

1. Remove lamb from the refrigerator and bring to room temperature, about 30 minutes.
2. Trim any pieces of surface fat from the lamb.
3. With a small sharp knife, cut 12–15 slits into the leg of lamb and stuff with slivered garlic cloves.
4. Pour vinegar over the lamb and season with salt and pepper.
5. Place lamb in the oven and roast 90–120 minutes or until a meat thermometer reads 71°C (160°F) for medium or 77°C (170°F) for well done.
6. Lightly tent with foil and let rest for 25 minutes before carving.
7. Serve with fluffy mashed potatoes, buttered green beans, broccoli, carrots and mint jelly.

"I love to put on this roast leg of lamb, invite all my crew of kids and grandkids, sit down and watch football all Sunday afternoon when the Indian Summer is in full bloom, uncork a nice bottle of Amarone, stir the fire and love every second of it."

"I love this recipe because it's easy and delicious any season, anytime."

Nicole Jones
Montreal, QC

Television Host, Reporter and Producer

ROSEMARY CHICKEN

SERVINGS 4 / PREPARATION 15 MIN / COOKING 1 H 15 MIN

INGREDIENTS

1 whole	chicken, without giblets
15 ml (1 tbsp)	salt
15 ml (1 tbsp)	ground black pepper
2	fresh rosemary sprigs
3	garlic cloves, peeled
1	lemon, halved

PREPARATION

Preheat the oven to 230°C (450°F)

1. Rinse chicken and pat it dry with paper towels.
2. Sprinkle with salt and pepper on each side. Rub half of the rosemary on the chicken.
3. Stuff the cavity with the second rosemary sprig, cloves of garlic and lemon halves. Place in a roasting pan.
4. Bake in the oven for about 1 hour. A meat thermometer should indicate at least 82°C (180°F).
5. Serve with grilled vegetables and sweet potatoes.

WINE PAIRING

LA CÔTE
CHARDONNAY
COTEAU ROUGEMONT

VIGNOBLE
ET CIDRERIE
COTEAU
ROUGEMONT

"The lookout point on Mount Royal is where I love to go to take in a view of the city!"

*"This dish reminds me of army cadet summer camps in Farnham.
It was the only tasty meal and the only meal served generously."*

SHEPHERD'S PIE

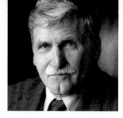

**Lieutenan General The Honourable
Roméo Dallaire** (Retired)
Montreal, QC

Senator and Founder,
Roméo Dallaire Child Soldiers Initiative

SERVINGS 4 / PREPARATION 20 MIN / COOKING 45 MIN

INGREDIENTS

1 L—1.25 L (4–5 cups)	potatoes, medium size
60 ml (¼ cup)	butter
125 ml (½ cup)	milk
1	onion, diced
454 g (1 lb)	ground beef
	Garlic salt
	Knorr Bovril liquid vegetable bouillon
284 ml (10 oz)	cream corn
284 ml (10 oz)	corn

PREPARATION

Preheat oven to 180°C (350°F)

1. Boil potatoes in salted water until tender. Drain.
2. Puree potatoes until smooth with the butter and milk.
3. In a skillet, brown the onion in butter. Add beef and garlic salt. Cook until golden brown.
4. Season with vegetable Bovril, to taste.
5. Lightly press the ground meat at the bottom of a 20 cm (8 in) square baking dish. Cover with the corn and the mashed potatoes.
6. Bake for about 30 minutes.

" *You can also top it with butter, an egg or cheese, to brown.* **"**

 "A place I find inspiring is Fort No. 1 in Levis overlooking the St. Lawrence River, across from the Citadelle of Quebec."

"When I lived in Singapore, I was inspired by their traditional & celebratory New Year's dish—Lo Hei. I brought it back to Canada and created my own. This dish is vegan and gluten free and the ingredients are available all year! In true Lo Hei fashion, I add a new ingredient every New Year to symbolize upgrading."

SINGAPOREAN STYLE SLAW

Susur Lee
Toronto, ON

Celebrity Chef

SERVINGS 4 / PREPARATION 30 MIN / COOKING 5 MIN

INGREDIENTS

1	pickled red onion
375 ml (1 ½ cups)	salted plum dressing
2	green onions, both white and green parts, julienned (cut into long thin strips, similar to matchsticks)
60 g (2 oz)	rice vermicelli, broken into 4 pieces
90 g (3 oz)	taro root, julienned
1	large English cucumber, julienned
1	large carrot, peeled, julienned
1	small jicama (yam bean), peeled, julienned
250 ml (1 cup)	winter radish, peeled, julienned
2	large Roma tomatoes, peeled, seeded, thinly sliced
20 ml (4 tsp)	sesame seeds, toasted
15 ml (1 tbsp)	pickled ginger
30 ml (6 tsp)	roasted peanuts, crushed
20 ml (4 tsp)	edible flower petals
20 ml (4 tsp)	fennel seedlings
20 ml (4 tsp)	purple basil seedlings
20 ml (4 tsp)	coriander seedlings
20 ml (4 tsp)	daikon sprouts
20 ml (4 tsp)	shallots, fried

Pickled Red Onion

1	red onion
250 ml (1 cup)	rice wine vinegar
250 ml (1 cup)	water
2 ml (½ tsp)	salt
1 ml (¼ tsp)	black peppercorns
1 ml (¼ tsp)	fennel seeds
1	bay leaf
1	sprig thyme

Salted Plum Dressing

250 ml (1 cup)	salted preserved plum, pitted
125 ml (½ cup)	rice wine vinegar
5 ml (1 tsp)	mirin (a rice wine similar to sake)
30 ml (2 tbsp)	onion oil
45 ml (3 tbsp)	sugar
2 ml (½ tsp)	fresh ginger, peeled, chopped
1 ml (¼ tsp)	sea salt

PREPARATION

Pickled Red Onion

1. Peel and julienne the red onion and set aside in a medium bowl.
2. In a small saucepan, bring vinegar and water to a boil. Season with salt, peppercorns, fennel seeds, bay leaf and thyme; continue boiling for another 5 minutes.
3. Pour mixture over onion while hot; let sit for 1 hour.

Salted Plum Dressing

1. In a blender, combine plum, vinegar, mirin, onion oil, sugar, ginger, and salt. Puree until smooth.

Singapore Slaw Salad

1. Soak green onion in very cold water to keep it crisp.
2. Meanwhile, heat a large pot of oil. When temperature reaches 204°C (400°F), deep fry the taro root, half the amount at a time, for 2 minutes until crisp and light gold. Remove slices from oil, place on a paper towel and lightly salt.
3. At the same temperature, quickly deep fry the vermicelli, half at a time, for 2 seconds, or until they curl. Remove from oil, place on a paper towel, and lightly salt.
4. Remove julienned green onion from the bowl and drain.
5. Divide the vermicelli equally between 4 plates and arrange green onion, cucumber, carrot, jicama, daikon, tomatoes, and pickled red onion around the noodles.
6. Top with fried taro root.
7. Sprinkle toasted sesame seeds and crushed peanuts over each salad.
8. In a small bowl, combine edible flower petals, seedlings, sprouts, and fried shallots. Sprinkle the flower-sprout-shallot mixture on salad.
9. Serve with salted plum dressing on the side.

*"Canada is a welcoming & multi-cultural country, so open minded and respectful of newcomers.
As a Chef, Canada is a playground of delicious seasonal ingredients from coast to coast and from sea to land.
What I love about Canada is the the connection between the rural & the urban. One of my favorite places is Fogo Island.
It's untouched & rich in history. It's what I imagine Canada's beginning to be. Then on the other hand, I also love TIFF
(Toronto International Film Festival). It brings so much arts & culture to my city. There's literally so much
diversity in Canada - I'm lucky to call it my home!"*

"This is my and my husband's favourite easy dinner to make, we usually have everything we need to make it, so we whip it up regularly and it is always satisfying and delicious."

SORT OF AMATRICIANA

Caitlin Cronenberg
Toronto, ON

Photographer

SERVINGS 2 / PREPARATION 15 MIN / COOKING 15 MIN

INGREDIENTS

1 package	dry fettuccine
	Olive oil
2	pancetta slices, 1.25 cm (½ in) thick, cut into chunks
	Butter
	Red pepper flakes
4	garlic cloves, minced
Small container	cherry tomatoes, rinsed, cut in halves, (separate a handful for garnish)
250 ml (1 cup)	Parmesan cheese, grated, plus extra for garnish
4–5	good leaves of basil, chopped (some reserved for garnish)
	Salt and pepper, to taste

PREPARATION

1. Set a large pot of salted water to boil. Cook pasta to package specifications for al dente; when draining, reserve some pasta water in a bowl.
2. Heat a large frying pan on medium-high heat. Add a good lug of olive oil and pancetta and cook until crispy. Remove to plate and set aside.
3. Add a bit more olive oil and a pat of butter to the pan, add pinch of red pepper flakes and garlic to the pan, cook until fragrant.
4. Add cherry tomatoes to the pan and lower heat to medium, let tomatoes begin to cook down.
5. Add about a half cup of pasta water to the pan and bring to simmer. Allow to simmer and allow tomatoes to cook down and reduce.
6. Add Parmesan cheese in handfuls, stirring after each addition. If it becomes too thick, add more pasta water.
7. Once sauce has thickened, return the cooked pancetta and add some basil. Stir.
8. Taste and season with salt and pepper as needed. I find the cheese and pancetta are quite salty so this doesn't need much, if any, but I like a lot of pepper.
9. Add pasta to the pan and toss to coat.
10. Serve immediately with some raw cherry tomatoes, fresh basil and cheese on top.

"I love spending time with my family at our country house in Caledon, Ontario."

"This is a Hamelin family secret recipe."

SPAGHETTI SAUCE

Charles & François Hamelin
Sainte-Julie, QC

Credit: M.A. L'Allier

Olympic Medallists in Speed Skating

SERVINGS 20–25 / PREPARATION 30 MIN / COOKING 5 H

INGREDIENTS

125 ml (½ cup)	oil
90 ml (6 tbsp)	butter
3 kg (6 lb)	ground beef

Step 1 Ingredients

1 kg (2 lb)	onions, chopped
2	leeks, chopped
2	green bell peppers, chopped

Step 2 Ingredients

1 kg (2 lb)	carrots, chopped
1	celery, chopped
1	garlic clove, chopped
90 ml (6 tbsp)	HP sauce (original)
60 ml (¼ cup)	Heinz 57 sauce
60 ml (¼ cup)	Worcestershire sauce
60 ml (¼ cup)	salt
30 ml (2 tbsp)	ground black pepper

Step 3 Ingredients

2.5 ml (½ tsp)	cayenne pepper
15 ml (3 tsp)	sugar
8	bay leaves
16 ml (3 ½ tsp)	marjoram
20 ml (4 tsp)	parsley, chopped

Step 4 Ingredients

5 ml (1 tsp)	chili pepper, ground
0.5 ml (⅛ tsp)	tabasco sauce
300 ml (1 ¼ cups)	chili sauce
300 ml (1 ¼ cups)	cream of tomato
570 ml (2 ⅓ cups)	tomato juice
390 ml (1 ½ cups)	tomato paste

PREPARATION

1. Heat the oil and butter in a large saucepan. Add the meat and cook through.
2. Add Step 1 and 2 ingredients, starting with the onions. Cook for 2 h 30 while mixing frequently.
3. Add Step 3 and 4 ingredients and cook for another 2 h 30, mixing frequently.

"We love maple products from l'Érable regional county. They are the pride of the area and of Quebec."

175

"I learned this recipe from other fishermen during a fishing trip."

SPICY BROWN SUGAR SALMON

**The Honourable
Philippe Couillard**
Saint-Félicien, QC

Premier of Quebec

SERVINGS 4 / PREPARATION 5 MIN / COOKING 20 MIN

INGREDIENTS

1	large salmon fillet
45 ml (3 tbsp)	maple syrup or rum, to taste
30 ml (2 tbsp)	brown sugar
15 ml (1 tbsp)	steak seasoning
	Vegetable side dish

PREPARATION

Preheat oven to 180°C (350°F)

1. Dry salmon fillet thoroughly.
2. Brush with maple syrup or rum, to taste.
3. Allow to dry again.
4. In a bowl, combine the brown sugar and steak seasoning; spread the mixture over the salmon.
5. Bake, skin face down, for a maximum of 20 minutes.
6. Brown the top of the fillet under the broiler.
7. Serve with grilled vegetables.

"My Canadian best is le Tour du Lac-Saint-Jean, Quebec."

*"This recipe is part of our family's heritage.
It is prepared and served mostly during the Christmas and New Year festivities."*

TOURTIERE

The Right Honourable
Paul Martin
Windsor, ON

21st Prime Minister of Canada

SERVINGS 10–12 (OR 2 PIES) / PREPARATION 15 MIN / COOKING 45 MIN

INGREDIENTS

1 kg (2 lb)	lean ground pork, shoulder
454 g (1 lb)	ground veal
1	onion, finely chopped
1 piece	butter
125 ml (½ cup)	very hot water
	Salt and pepper
	Cinnamon, to taste
	Bread crumbs
1	egg, beaten

PREPARATION

Preheat the oven to 220°C (425°F)

1. Prepare pastry of your choice.
2. In a large skillet, add butter and onion; sauté for a few minutes.
3. Add pork and veal, sauté 8–10 minutes, until it's no longer pink.
4. Add hot water and season with salt and pepper, to taste.
5. Lower the heat, cover and let cook for about 20 minutes.
6. Remove fat, if necessary, and add some bread crumbs for a nice texture.
7. Add cinnamon, to taste and adjust seasoning.
8. Thoroughly mash the meat mixture with a potato pestle; let cool.
9. Pour the meat mixture into 2 pastries; cover with top pastry and brush top pastry with the beaten egg.
10. Make a hole in the centre of each pie.
11. Bake in the oven for 10 minutes.
12. Lower the heat to 180°C (350°F) and continue baking 25–30 minutes or until nice and golden.
13. Let rest 5 minutes before serving.

"Maple products found in many areas throughout the country and especially in Quebec have always been my favourite Canadian products. I also love the LaSalle Rapids, a place with which I have developed a certain bond. It is rich in history on the early explorations of North America. I found myself in this area many times when I was representing the LaSalle-Émard municipalities in the House of Commons."

"This recipe was found among the medals and rosaries at the Cistercian abbey of Fontfroide in Languedoc Roussillon (15 km from Narbonne). It has welcomed pilgrims travelling to Saint-Jacques-de-Compostelle for centuries."

VEAL BLANQUETTE

Bernard Derome
Montreal, QC

Former Radio-Canada Television Anchor

SERVINGS 4 / PREPARATION 30 MIN / COOKING 1 H

INGREDIENTS

1 kg (2 lb)	veal, middle cut breast, 1ˢᵗ rib and shoulder, coarsely cubed
	Nice amount of unsalted lard, cubed
2	carrots, sliced
1	onion or 2 French shallots, peeled
2	garlic buds, peeled
	Mushrooms, sliced (optional)
30 ml (2 tbsp)	flour
2	bouillon cubes, chicken or vegetable
	Salt and pepper
1	egg yolk
1	lemon, juice

PREPARATION

1. In a casserole, brown the lard, carrots, onion, garlic and mushrooms.
2. Add salt and pepper to veal and add to casserole and brown.
3. Sprinkle with flour and cover with water.
4. Add bouillon cubes, pepper and let simmer for 60 minutes.
5. In a bowl, whisk together the yolk, 1 ladle of sauce and lemon juice.
6. Add to sauce and mix well. Let cook for 10 minutes.
7. Serve with rice or egg pasta.

"We can never fully realize how much Canada is a country of great freedom! Be aware of that!"

"This recipe is a combination of dishes I ate while in India and Southeast Asia. When I prepare it, it takes me right back to the ambiance of my travels!"

VEGETABLE CURRY

Geneviève Borne
Quebec City, QC

Television Host

SERVINGS 2 / PREPARATION 20 MIN / COOKING 15 MIN

INGREDIENTS

30 ml (2 tbsp)	coconut oil
1	zucchini, cut into strips
1	red bell pepper, cut into strips
1	sweet potato, cut into strips
1	can of coconut milk
½	can of chickpeas
1	lemon, juice
15 ml (1 tbsp)	curry powder
2	kaffir lime leaves
	Basmati rice

PREPARATION

1. In a large skillet, heat oil and add vegetables. Sauté for a few minutes.
2. Add coconut milk, chick peas, curry powder, lemon juice and kaffir lime leaves.
3. Let simmer for 15 minutes.
4. Serve on basmati rice or as is.

❝ *Bon appétit!* ❞

 "My favourite place in Canada is the Mackenzie King Estate in Ottawa. Quite peculiar and rich in history, this place was the estate of the former Prime Minister of Canada. He collected the ruins of destroyed or burned buildings and scattered them on his land. Arches, statues and columns trace an enchanting journey through the gardens."

"The recipe has been passed down from our Grandma so, we call it Weir Family Lasagna Recipe."

WEIR FAMILY LASAGNA

Mike Weir
Bright's Grove, ON

Masters Champion, Professional Golfer

SERVINGS 6–8 / PREPARATION 30 MIN / COOKING 1 H 10

INGREDIENTS

Tomato Sauce

796 ml (28 oz)	crushed tomatoes
156 ml (5.5 oz)	tomato paste
156 ml (5.5 oz)	water
15 ml (1 tbsp)	sugar
2 ml (¼ tsp)	salt
2 ml (¼ tsp)	pepper
3 ml (½ tsp)	garlic salt
5 ml (1 tsp)	oregano
2	bay leaves
60 ml (¼ cup)	Parmesan cheese, grated
30 ml (2 tbsp)	fresh basil

Meat Filling

454 g (1 lb)	ground beef
225 g (½ lb)	ground pork
454 g (1 lb)	hot Italian sausage
2	eggs
2 ml (¼ tsp)	salt
2 ml (¼ tsp)	pepper
3 ml (½ tsp)	garlic salt or powder
30 ml (2 tbsp)	fresh parsley, chopped
2	cloves garlic
125 ml (½ cup)	Italian-style bread crumbs
60 ml (¼ cup)	Parmesan cheese

Other Ingredients

454 g (1 lb)	ricotta cheese
1	egg
5 ml (1 tsp)	sugar
15 ml (1 tbsp)	parsley, chopped
30 ml (2 tbsp)	Parmesan cheese
1 pinch	salt and pepper
1 package	Olivieri lasagna sheets
750 ml (3 cups)	mozzarella cheese, shredded
500 ml (2 cups)	Parmesan cheese, shredded

PREPARATION

Preheat oven to 180°C (350°F)

Tomato Sauce

1. Combine all ingredients in sauce pan and bring to a boil. Reduce heat and simmer for 1 hour.

Meat Filling

1. Hand mix all ingredients, except sausage, sprinkle with water and let sit in the refrigerator for 1 hour.
2. Form meat mixture in desired size balls. Fry meatballs in olive oil and garlic until brown.
3. Cut sausage links into 5 cm (2 in) pieces and fry in olive oil until brown.
4. Place all meat in the tomato sauce and let simmer for 1 hour.

Assembly

1. Mix ricotta cheese with egg, sugar, parsley, Parmesan cheese, salt and pepper.
2. Remove 10 meatballs and 5 sausage pieces from sauce and mash and blend, repeat as required.
3. Spread generous helping of sauce to the bottom of a lightly greased pan; 23 x 33–cm (9 x 13–inch).
4. Layer lasagna sheets, cut to fit pan.
5. Spread ricotta mix on lasagna sheets.
6. Spread meat filling on top.
7. Spread mozzarella cheese generously.
8. Spread tomato sauce.
9. Sprinkle with Parmesan cheese.
10. Place another layer of lasagna sheets; repeat previous steps.
11. Finish with last layer of lasagna sheets. Cover with tomato sauce, mozzarella and Parmesan cheeses.
12. Cover with foil and bake 45–60 minutes.
13. Remove foil and bake for 10 more minutes.
14. Let stand 15 minutes and serve.

"I have been lucky enough to visit every province in Canada and love each one for different reasons; but my home town of Bright's Grove holds a special place for me, with its beautiful beaches, small-town atmosphere, friendly people and its proximity to the Niagara region, where I have family members."

ICE FISHING VILLAGE – LA BAIE, QC

DESSERTS

"The original recipe is from the 'Complete Harrowsmith Cookbook', but my mom and I have modified it over the years. I only bake once a year, at Christmas. This is what I make."

ALMOND SHORTBREAD

Sophie Lui
Vancouver, BC

Co-Anchor, Global News Hour at 6

SERVINGS 4 DOZEN / PREPARATION 10 MIN / COOKING 30 MIN

INGREDIENTS

454 g (1 lb)	butter, softened
500 ml (2 cups)	all-purpose flour
250 ml (1 cup)	corn starch
250 ml (1 cup)	icing sugar

Optional

150 g (⅓ lb)	sliced almonds
	Dried cranberries (to garnish)

PREPARATION

Preheat oven to 150°C (300°F)

1. In a bowl, combine flour, corn starch and icing sugar.
2. In a large bowl, use electric mixer to whip the butter.
3. Add dry ingredients, half a cup at a time, whipping each into butter mixture
   It's easier to add a small amount of dry ingredients at a time so that you don't have a flour explosion all over your kitchen.
4. When dough is mixed, stir in almonds.
5. Roll mixture into small balls—about 15 ml (1 tbsp) per cookie—and place on a baking sheet lined with parchment paper.
6. Flatten slightly with a fork, just enough to see a little mark from the fork tines.
7. Add a few dried cranberries in the centre of each cookie.
8. Bake 25–30 minutes, or until edges are golden.
9. Let the cookies cool; dust with icing sugar.

♡ *"I was born and raised in Vancouver and my favourite thing to do in Canada is walk along the beach in Tofino, BC, rain or shine."*

"This is my aunt Marguerite's easy recipe! Marguerite was my mother's youngest sister and a wonderful cook. I wanted to pay tribute to her. One day, I phoned her because I had 7 croissants that had become a little too dry but that I didn't want to throw away. She gave me some directions and voilà! This delicious dessert was born!"

AUNT MARGUERITE'S SIMPLE DELIGHT

Marina Orsini
Ville-Émard, QC

Actress, Radio and Television Host

SERVINGS 16 / PREPARATION 15 MIN

INGREDIENTS

8	slightly dry croissants, broken into pieces
250 ml (1 cup)	15% country-style cream
500 ml (2 cups)	35% country-style cream
60 ml (¼ cup)	maple syrup or more
	Fresh berries (blueberries, strawberries, raspberries, boysenberries, etc.)
	Icing sugar

PREPARATION

Prepare in the morning, ideally, so it has time to soak.

1. Whip 35% country-style cream and gently fold in maple syrup; set aside.
2. Place the croissants in a 23 x 30 x 10 cm (9 x 12 x 4 in) glass or porcelain serving dish.
3. Splash with 15% country-style cream.
4. Add a layer of berries.
5. Add a layer of whipped cream.
6. Repeat steps 3 and 4 and finish the last layer with berries.
7. Sprinkle with icing sugar.
8. Refrigerate all afternoon.
9. Serve cold. Yum!

" *Easy and guaranteed success!* "

"Quebec City has always been a place of choice to me so much that I dream of having a pied-à-terre in the city some day. I also very much like Toronto which I recently discovered. Wonderful city!"

"A delicious healthy recipe I discovered at
Les Serres et Aliments Bien-Être et Bon Goût in Montreal, Quebec."

BLUEBERRY AND KALE ENERGY BALLS

Annie Dufresne
Quebec City, QC

Actress and Singer

SERVINGS 30–36 / PREPARATION 30 MIN

INGREDIENTS

500 ml (2 cups)	dates
500 ml (2 cups)	almonds, crushed into small pieces
250 ml (1 cup)	fresh blueberries, crushed
250 ml (1 cup)	grated coconut
500 ml (2 cups)	young kale, finely chopped
125 ml (½ cup)	hemp seeds

PREPARATION

1. Put dates and some water in a food processor and mix into a paste. Set aside in a large bowl.
2. Add all remaining ingredients except the hemp seeds and mix well until combined.
3. With a small ice cream scoop or with your hands, form balls with the mixture.
4. Coat with hemp seeds and place on a tray.

   Optional: Put in a dehydrator at low temperature for 20 minutes. It will make the balls less sticky.
5. Freeze.
6. Thaw 1 hour before eating.

"I love the insular world of Îles de la Madeleine, a place where time stands still."

"I love blueberries from Nova Scotia or Sudbury, two of my favourite places. The recipe is from my wife, Janet."

BLUEBERRY CRISP

Arthur B. McDonald
Sydney, NS

Professor Emeritus, Queen's University,
2015 Nobel Physics Laureate

SERVINGS 4–6 / PREPARATION 15 MIN / COOKING 40 MIN

INGREDIENTS

500 ml (2 cups)	Nova Scotia or Sudbury blueberries
5 ml (1 tsp)	ground nutmeg
5 ml (1 tsp)	ground cinnamon
15 ml (1 tbsp)	grated orange or lemon rind
250 ml (1 cup)	flour or gluten-free flour
250 ml (1 cup)	oatmeal
125 ml (½ cup)	melted butter or margarine
125 ml (½ cup)	brown sugar
1 pinch	salt

PREPARATION

Preheat the oven to 180°C (350°F)

1. Place blueberries in loaf pan. Sprinkle nutmeg, cinnamon and orange or lemon rind over berries.
2. Put flour and oatmeal into a mixing bowl.
3. Add brown sugar and melted butter (or margarine) and mix together into a crumbled state.
4. Spread on top of berry mixture.
5. Bake for 40 minutes.
6. Serve warm with ice cream, whipped cream or half and half cream (lactose free).

"I love blueberry season in Canada. When we were building the Sudbury Neutrino Observatory there were enormous numbers of blueberries near our offices. Each season I had a bouquet of fresh blueberries in a cup on my desk, ripe and delicious."

"This is my mom's famous apple pie recipe."

CAROL'S DELUXE APPLE PIE

Jennifer Jones
Winnipeg, MB

Olympic Medallist in Women's Curling

SERVINGS 8 / PREPARATION 20 MIN / COOKING 30–45 MIN

INGREDIENTS

Pastry

1	egg
5 ml (1 tsp)	vinegar
1.25 L (5 cups)	flour
15 ml (1 tsp)	baking powder
75 ml (⅓ cup)	white sugar
5 ml (1 tsp)	salt
454 g (1 lb)	Tenderflake lard, cut into pieces
180 ml (¾ cup)	milk, approximately

Filling

1.5 L (6 cups)	apples, peeled, sliced thin
90 ml (6 tbsp)	granulated sugar
90 ml (6 tbsp)	brown sugar
75 ml (⅓ cup)	flour
15 ml (1 tbsp)	cinnamon
1.25 ml (¼ tsp)	salt
60 ml (¼ cup)	butter
5 ml (1 tsp)	lemon juice

PREPARATION

Preheat oven to 220°C—230 °C (425°F–450°F)

Pastry

1. Break up the egg slightly with vinegar; add milk to make 250 ml (1 cup) of liquid.
2. Mix dry ingredients and add them to a blender; add lard and mix.
3. Add liquid and knead the mix together.
4. Chill in the fridge while preparing the apples.
5. When ingredients are ready, roll out the pastry.

Filling and Assembly

1. Peel and slice apples.
2. Combine sugars, flour, cinnamon and salt together.
3. Mix with sliced apples.
4. Spread apple mixture into unbaked pastry shell.
5. Dot with butter, sprinkle with lemon juice.
6. Cover with top pastry crust, sealing carefully and making slits in the pastry cover to allow steam to escape.
7. Bake in hot oven for 10 minutes. Reduce heat to 180°C (350°F) and continue baking 20–30 minutes until apples are cooked.

❝ *Enjoy!* **❞**

*"My life has been shaped by competing in many small town curling rinks across Canada.
The people I have met are what makes Canada so great! I also love any moment I spend with my family
on the beautiful Georgian Bay, in Ontario."*

"I adapted an original recipe from my Olympic teammate, Catherine Ward."

CARROT CAKE WITH MAPLE CREAM CHEESE ICING

Caroline Ouellette
Montreal, QC

Credit: Rémy Boily

Olympic Medallist in Women's Hockey

SERVINGS 12 / PREPARATION 30 MIN / COOKING 35 MIN

INGREDIENTS

Cake

500 ml (2 cups)	all-purpose flour
10 ml (2 tsp)	baking soda
5 ml (1 tsp)	salt
15 ml (1 tbsp)	ground cinnamon
250 ml (1 cup)	sugar
250 ml (1 cup)	pineapple, in its own juice
180 ml (¾ cup)	canola oil
4	large eggs
1 L (4 cups)	grated peeled carrots
30 ml (2 tbsp)	minced peeled ginger
250 ml (1 cup)	toasted shredded coconut for decoration on the cake

Icing

350 g (12 oz)	cream cheese, at room temperature
45 ml (3 tbsp)	unsalted butter, at room temperature
625 ml (2 ½ cups)	powdered sugar
60 ml (¼ cup)	pure maple syrup

PREPARATION

Preheat oven to 180°C (350°F)

Cake

1. Butter two 22 cm (9 in)–diameter cake pans.
2. Whisk flour, baking soda, salt and cinnamon in a medium bowl.
3. Whisk sugar and oil in a large bowl until well blended.
4. Whisk in the eggs one at a time..
5. Add flour mixture and stir until blended. Stir in the carrots, pineapple and ginger.
6. Divide the batter between the two prepared pans.
7. Bake the cakes until a knife inserted into the center comes out clean; about 35 minutes.
8. Cool cakes in pans 15 minutes.
9. Cool cakes completely.

Icing

1. Using an electric mixer, beat the cream cheese and butter in a large bowl until light and fluffy.
2. Add powdered sugar and beat at low speed until well blended.
3. Beat in maple syrup. Chill until just firm enough to spread, 30 minutes.
4. Place 1 cake layer on a platter. Spread with 180 ml (¾ cup) icing.
5. Top with a second layer. Spread remaining icing over entire cake. Sprinkle toasted coconut on top.
6. Let stand at room temperature 30 minutes before serving.

> " *I hope you enjoy this dessert as much as I have in times of celebrations!* "

"The best thing to do in Canada is to play hockey. I have the privilege of playing for Les Canadiennes de Montréal with the Canadian Women's Hockey League. This season we played at the Bell Centre for the first time in our history, winning 1-0 against Calgary in front of 6,000 fans. On March 5, 2017, we won the greatest award in our sport in Canada, the Clarkson Cup, beating the Calgary Inferno 3-1. It was the fourth Clarkson Cup for our organization."

*"This is my grandmother Thérèse's recipe.
She used to make the very best white cakes in the world!"*

DELECTABLE WHITE CAKE WITH ÎLE D'ORLÉANS STRAWBERRIES

Jean-Philippe Wauthier
La Baie, QC

TV and Radio Show Host

SERVINGS 12–16 / PREPARATION 10 MIN / COOKING 30–40 MIN

INGREDIENTS

4	eggs
500 ml (2 cups)	sugar
10 ml (2 tsp)	vanilla
500 ml (2 cups)	unbleached white flour
10 ml (2 tsp)	baking powder
1 pinch	salt
250 ml (1 cup)	warm milk to which 30 ml (2 tbsp) butter is added
	Île d'Orléans strawberries or other variety
	35% cream, whipped

PREPARATION

Preheat the oven to 190°C (375°F)

1. Grease and flour two 17 cm (8 in) diameter baking tins.
2. With a mixer, beat eggs, sugar and vanilla until fluffy.
3. Reduce the speed of the mixer; add flour, baking powder and salt while beating.
4. Fold in warm milk with a spatula.
5. Pour mixture into the tins.
6. Bake in the oven 30–40 minutes or until a toothpick inserted into the cake comes out clean.
7. Serve with whipped cream and flavourful Île d'Orléans strawberries!

"My Canadian favourites are the restaurant Petite Maison in Montreal and the beautiful city of La Baie, Quebec."

"To me, this cookie is what the holidays are all about, I only make them at this time of year, and I used to send them to my kids when they were away at school before the holidays. They're sweet but with a little spice. They're a grown-up classic, but you can make them fun for little ones with some coloured sprinkles."

The Honourable Kathleen Wynne
Toronto, ON

Premier of Ontario

GINGER SNAPS

6–8 DOZEN / PREPARATION 15 MIN / COOKING 12 MIN

INGREDIENTS

180 ml (¾ cup)	butter
500 ml (2 cups)	sugar
2	eggs, well beaten
125 ml (½ cup)	molasses
10 ml (2 tsp)	vinegar
930 ml (3 ¾ cups)	all-purpose flour
7 ml (1 ½ tsp)	baking soda
10—15 ml (2–3 tsp)	ground ginger
2 ml (½ tsp)	ground cinnamon
1 ml (¼ tsp)	ground cloves

PREPARATION

Preheat oven to 163°C (325°F)

1. Cream butter and sugar.
2. Stir in all other ingredients. Mix until blended.
3. Form dough into 2 cm (¾ in) balls. I dip one side of each ball in coloured sprinkles before I put them on the cookie sheet.
4. Bake on a greased cookie sheet for about 12 minutes. Could be less than that, depending on the heat of your oven. If the cookies flatten out and their tops start to crack, then they are ready.

" I have also used margarine.

I only use a little over 750 ml (3 cups) of all-purpose flour, which makes the cookies chewy, and not rock-hard.

I use at least 15 ml (3 tsp) of ground ginger.

I also add about 5 ml (¼ tsp) salt because I always bake with unsalted butter or margarine. "

"I have always felt a sense of possibility about the great things Canadians can do together. We created a publicly funded health-care system, a national pension plan and the Charter of Rights and Freedoms. And we have become the model of diversity and inclusiveness that the world needs today."

"This recipe has been my favourite since I was a little kid. I believe, back in the 1960's, E.D. Smith used to put the recipe on the side of the can and it is a sure-fire winner. My mother STILL makes it for me every time there is a special occasion. Why mess with a good thing?"

LAFLAMME FAMILY CHEESECAKE

Lisa LaFlamme
Kitchener, ON

Chief News Anchor and Senior Editor
CTV NATIONAL NEWS

SERVINGS 6–8 / PREPARATION 15 MIN

INGREDIENTS

Crust

625 ml (2 ½ cups)	graham crackers (rolled)
125 ml (½ cup)	brown sugar
125 ml (½ cup)	melted butter

Filling

1 small package	Dream Whip
125 ml (½ cup)	milk
3 ml (½ tsp)	vanilla
225 g (8 oz)	cream cheese
250 ml (1 cup)	icing sugar

Topping

590 ml (20 oz)	cherry pie filling

PREPARATION

1. Mix crust ingredients and press evenly along the bottom of a rectangular Pyrex baking dish.
2. Whip Dream Whip, milk, and vanilla in one bowl, as directed.
3. In a separate bowl, mix softened cream cheese and icing sugar.
4. Gently combine Dream Whip mixture and cheese mixture.
5. Spread over graham crust.
6. Spoon cherry filling over cheese mixture.
7. Allow to set for 12 hours in the refrigerator before serving.

" *It keeps for several days.* **"**

"At the cottage, my favourite thing to do is watch the sun go down from the shores of Lake Huron. I've been doing it all my life and it only gets more beautiful."

"This is my mother's recipe; she was an excellent cook. She helped my father with the family business and worked at night, so her recipes had to be delicious and above all, quick and easy to execute. When I was little I was fascinated by the egg whites forming into white peaks."

MY MOM'S
DELICIOUS MAPLE MOUSSE

Monique F. Leroux
Montreal, QC

President, International Co-operative Alliance

SERVINGS 12 / PREPARATION 5 MIN

INGREDIENTS

500 ml (2 cups)	maple syrup
4	fresh egg whites

PREPARATION

1. In a bowl, beat egg whites until stiff peaks form.
2. In a saucepan, boil the syrup 5–10 minutes. It must rise in bubbles and fall back. The temperature shouldn't go over 121°C (250°F) on a candy thermometer.
3. Gently pour the boiling maple syrup over the egg whites while whisking the mixture continuously.
4. Pour in a large serving bowl.
5. Refrigerate until it is time to serve. (You may have to whisk the mixture before serving if the syrup has separated from the whites.)

"A few of my numerous Canadian favourites: the beautiful St-Lawrence River on which I have sailed… and my home on the shore of Lake Massawippi, with my feet in the water, gazing at the sun setting on the mountains."

*"From the Mennonite Treasury of Recipes.
I've been making this for family birthday cakes since I was a kid."*

NEVER FAIL CHOCOLATE CAKE

Dawna Friesen
Vancouver, BC

Anchor, Global National

SERVINGS 8–12 / PREPARATION 10 MIN / COOKING 30 MIN

INGREDIENTS

30 ml (2 tbsp)	butter, melted
150 ml (⅔ cup)	cocoa
250 ml (1 cup)	white sugar
250 ml (1 cup)	flour
8 ml (1 ½ tsp)	baking powder
8 ml (1 ½ tsp)	baking soda
1 ml (¼ tsp)	salt
1	egg
150 ml (⅔ cup)	milk
5 ml (1 tsp)	vanilla

PREPARATION

Preheat oven to 180°C (350°F)

1. In a bowl, combine white sugar, flour, baking powder, baking soda and salt.
2. Break the egg into a 250 ml (1 cup) measuring cup and add enough milk to fill.
3. Mix melted butter with cocoa.
4. Add milk and egg to dry ingredients and mix.
5. Add melted butter and cocoa combination with vanilla and mix well.
6. Pour into well-greased 20–cm (8–inch) square pan and bake for about 30 minutes.

"I grew up on a farm west of Winnipeg and love the prairies… the big sky, the smell of harvest and stunning stars on a clear night. It's got a special place in my heart, and I treasure my copy of the Mennonite Treasury of Recipes because it reminds me of my heritage and especially of my mum, who taught me how to bake."

"This is the cake I used to ask my mother for my birthday during my teenage years. The source is unknown but my brother, Ricardo, adapted it."

QUEEN ELIZABETH CAKE

Martine Mai
Montreal, QC

Singer

SERVINGS 16 / PREPARATION 15 MIN / COOKING 25–30 MIN

INGREDIENTS

Cake

250 ml (1 cup)	water
250 ml (1 cup)	dates, pitted, coarsely chopped
2.5 ml (½ tsp)	baking soda
430 ml (1 ¾ cups)	all-purpose flour, sifted
8 ml (1 ½ tsp)	baking powder
1 pinch	salt
125 ml (½ cup)	unsalted butter, softened
180 ml (¾ cup)	brown sugar
2	eggs

Icing

125 ml (½ cup)	35% cream
125 ml (½ cup)	unsalted butter
375 ml (1 ½ cups)	brown sugar
375 ml (1 ½ cups)	unsweetened shredded coconut

PREPARATION

Preheat oven to 180°C (350°F)—with rack in the middle position

Cake

1. Line a 25 cm (10 in) springform pan with parchment paper or a square 23 cm (9 in) Pyrex cake pan. Butter and flour the sides.
2. In a saucepan, bring water, dates and baking soda to a boil. Let simmer, stirring frequently, for about 3 minutes. Let cool and set aside.
3. In a bowl, combine flour, baking powder and salt; set aside.
4. In another bowl, cream the butter and brown sugar with an electric mixer.
5. Add eggs, one at a time, and beat until smooth.
6. At low speed, add dry ingredients alternately with the warm date mixture; pour into pan.
7. Bake in the oven 25–30 minutes or until a toothpick inserted in the centre of the cake comes out clean.
8. Place cake on a baking sheet, if desired, to collect excess that could spill.
9. Turn the oven to broil.

Icing

1. In a saucepan, bring all ingredients to a boil, stirring constantly. Simmer gently for about 2 minutes.
2. Spread icing on the warm cake and bake for an additional 2–3 minutes or until lightly golden.

"In Canada, we have access to beautiful national parks and for the last few years, I have been happy to live near one of them: the magnificent Mont-Saint-Bruno Park, Quebec. Miles of trails to discover, a daily appointment with beauty!"

"When I was a kid, we used to go to my grandmother Lafleur's for dinner every Sunday. With the uncles, aunts, and cousins, we were more than 40 people. There was always a ton of desserts, including the famous raspberry pie. I love this pie; I could eat a whole one by myself."

RASPBERRY PIE

Guy Lafleur
Thurso, QC

Former NHL Hockey Player

SERVINGS 8 / PREPARATION 30 MIN / COOKING 1 H

INGREDIENTS

Crust

454 g (1 lb)	Tenderflake shortening
10 ml (2 tsp)	salt
1	egg
15 ml (1 tbsp)	vinegar
250 ml (1 cup)	iced water
1 L (4 cups)	flour

Topping

1 L (4 cups)	raspberries
250 ml (1 cup)	sugar

PREPARATION

1. Place shortening and salt in a large mixing bowl.
2. Beat the egg in a measuring cup. Add vinegar and iced water. Pour mixture over shortening and salt. Add 750 ml (3 cups) of flour. Prepare fourth cup and set aside.
3. Thoroughly combine the shortening, flour and egg mixture. The dough will be very sticky. Add fourth cup of flour and knead until combined. If the dough is still too sticky, add a little flour. Because there are only 1 L (4 cups) of flour in this recipe, you can use all the flour you need when rolling the dough. Makes approximately 4 pies; unused dough can be frozen.
4. Roll out the dough into two 23 cm (9 in) disks. Line a pie plate with pastry.
5. In a large bowl, combine the raspberries and sugar by tossing. Spread in the pastry.
6. Brush the edges of the dough with water and top with second pastry. Tightly seal the edges and make a few incisions. To create a golden colour and sheen, you can brush with egg wash, a mixture made of a beaten egg yolk and a little water.
7. Bake at 200°C (400°F) for 10 minutes. Lower oven to 180°C (350°F) and continue baking 45–60 minutes or until golden.

"I love flying my helicopter. It's one of my favourite hobbies. I often fly to Thurso to see my mother. Every time I go she bakes my favourite dessert: a raspberry pie."

"Brought to Canada by my mother, Jean Bowman, when she immigrated to Montreal in 1930. She always made shortbread for us at Christmas and special occasions. She used cookie cut-outs and also made the shortbread into large rounds [about 15–cm (6–inch) across] circles and pricked them with a fork for decoration."

SCOTT'S SHORTBREAD

Scotty Bowman
Verdun, QC

Former NHL Head Coach

SERVINGS 12 / PREPARATION 30 MIN / COOKING 15–20 MIN

INGREDIENTS

225 g (½ lb)	soft butter
180 ml (¾ cup)	sugar
430 ml (1 ¾ cups)	flour
1	egg yolk
1 pinch	salt

PREPARATION

Preheat oven to 180°C (350°F)

1. In a bowl, mix butter and sugar until light and fluffy.
2. Add egg yolk and salt, beat until smooth.
3. Gradually add flour and mix until well blended.
4. Pour mixture out on a board and roll to desired thickness. Leave dough at least 1 cm (½ in) thick, since it does not rise.
5. Cut with a cookie cutter and bake 15–20 minutes on an ungreased cookie sheet until light brown. Watch it carefully. Do not let get too brown.

 "We love to cross over the border for dinner to enjoy Canadian Chinese food, Swiss Chalet and Montreal smoked meat. When we return to Montreal, still one of our favourite cities, we love visiting Mount Royal, the Laurentian Mountains and the Eastern Townships where we had a small hobby farm in the 1970s. And, of course, returning to my home town in Verdun, Quebec."

"So I'm a huge pie lover, and I mean huge. I guess my boyhood Canadian roots make me love my favourite Strawberry Rhubarb Pie. We don't have pie in Trinidad where I was born but when we moved to Canada, to the small Albertan town of Edson, I was 5, and rhubarb was growing everywhere."

STRAWBERRY RHUBARB PIE

Sean Cheesman
Edson, AB

Dancer and Choreographer

SERVINGS 8 / PREPARATION 15 MIN / COOKING 35–40 MIN

INGREDIENTS

250 ml (1 cup)	white sugar
125 ml (½ cup)	all-purpose flour
454 g (1 lb)	fresh rhubarb, chopped
675 g (1 ½ lb)	fresh strawberries
1	recipe *pastry for a 22 cm (9 in) double crust pie
30 ml (2 tbsp)	butter
1	egg yolk
30 ml (2 tbsp)	white sugar

*A pastry recipe can be found on page 213.

PREPARATION

Preheat oven to 200°C (400°F)

1. In a large bowl, mix flour and sugar. Add strawberries and chopped rhubarb. Toss with sugar and flour; let stand for 30 minutes.
2. Pour filling into the pie crust. Dot top with butter, and cover with top crust. Use water to seal the edges of top and bottom crust together.
3. Brush yolk on the top of pie using a pastry brush. Sprinkle with sugar. Cut small holes in top of the crust to let steam escape.
4. Bake 35–40 minutes, or until bubbling and brown.
5. Cool on a rack before serving.

"My favourite things to do in Canada besides seeing old friends and family is all about food: French fries with gravy, Old Dutch salt & vinegar chips, Real Fruit gummies and fudge from Banff."

"This sweet potato bread is a generous and delectable dessert that takes me back to the most beautiful moments of my childhood in Haiti. It reminds me of my native land's daytime and night time tropical scents, of my mother's bursts of laughter, of her enveloping gaze and of her great sense of sharing and celebrations. I recommend brown sugar in place of corn syrup and why not maple syrup, for a boreal accent! Delicious! We always ask for more!"

SWEET POTATO BREAD

The Right Honourable Michaëlle Jean
Ottawa, ON

Secretary General of La Francophonie

Credit : Cyril Bailleul

SERVINGS 10–12 / PREPARATION 25 MIN / COOKING 1 H 30 MIN

INGREDIENTS

80 ml (⅓ cup)	butter, melted
1 kg (2 lb) 4–5	sweet potatoes, peeled, cut in four
1	banana, very ripe
3	eggs
250 ml (1 cup)	sugar
180 ml (¾ cup)	corn syrup
90 ml (6 tbsp)	coconut milk
90 ml (6 tbsp)	Eagle Brand sweetened condensed milk
2 ml (¼ tsp)	vanilla extract
2 ml (¼ tsp)	ground cinnamon
2 ml (¼ tsp)	ground nutmeg
45 g (¼ cup)	raisins

PREPARATION

Preheat oven to 180°C (350°F)

1. Grease a bread pan and sprinkle with flour; set aside.
2. Cook potatoes in salted water until soft; drain and let cool.
3. In a blender, add the potatoes and banana; puree.
4. Add remaining ingredients and mix well until a homogeneous mixture is obtained.
5. Pour the mixture into the prepared pan and bake for 90 minutes.
6. Let cool in pan for about 10 minutes; place on a rack and let cool fully.
7. Serve cold with Coquimol, a coconut cream sauce.

" *Don't expect a cake-like texture. This sweet potato bread is more like a flan.* **"**

"I love Nahanni National Park, about 600 km west of Yellowknife. This park is home to Virginia Falls, which is almost three times higher than the Niagara Falls, which flow into the South Nahanni River and is spectacularly magnificent. A descent of the river by canoe is an unforgettable adventure."

"This is the yummiest of desserts and very healthy too, although wonderfully rich! Easy to make in no time at all, and all in one cast iron pan! How fitting for celebrating Canada's 150th!"

Bonnie Brooks
Toronto, ON

Former Chair of the LCBO

TARTE TATIN FOR CANADA'S 150TH

SERVINGS 6–8 / PREPARATION 15 MIN / COOKING 45 MIN

INGREDIENTS

6	apples, use tart apples like Granny Smith
½	lemon for juice
90 ml (6 tbsp)	butter
3 large drops	vanilla extract (get a nice Jamaican or Spice Islands one, as it's good for Christmas too!)
325 ml (1 ⅓ cups)	brown sugar, natural (divided into 250 ml (1 cup) and 75 ml (⅓ cup) separately)
Puff pastry	frozen, bought anywhere in rolls that roll into two sheets—defrost 1–2 hours at room temperature. These will be your crust!

PREPARATION

Preheat oven to 200°C (400°F)

1. Peel, core and cut the apples in beautiful regular quarters, and toss with the juice from half of the lemon in a large bowl.
2. Add vanilla extract.
3. Add 75 ml (⅓ cup) sugar and swirl around to sweat the apples; leave for 10 minutes.
4. Melt butter in a 23 or 25 cm (9 or10 in) round cast iron frying pan for both stovetop cooking and for oven cooking. Add 250 ml (1 cup) brown sugar to caramelize over low heat. Watch so it doesn't burn—will turn rich and gooey and thicker.
5. Add apples to the caramel and layer with your fingers in a nice pattern as you will flip this upside down later and will see the apple pattern.
6. Turn on the stove again and heat for 20 more minutes, basting occasionally the juices overtop of the apples and pressing down on apples regularly.
7. When apples feel softer but not soggy, take them off the stove and cool. Ensure there isn't too much liquid or it will be messy when it flips over later. Spoon some off if necessary.
8. Take the puff pastry, unroll it and put the two layers, one at a time, on the fry pan to seal around edges. Pat down onto the apples, so the two square sheets overlap and cross over each other, with 4–6 triangles on the sides falling over. This looks great when it puffs up after it cooks.
9. Make 4 slashes in the top of the pastry to release steam.
10. Place in the oven for 15 minutes and watch so it doesn't burn.
11. Take out, cool down, and when ready to eat, flip over quickly by holding your serving plate over the fry pan and flipping it upside down—an amazing look!

❝ *Enjoy!* **❞**

"What I enjoy most about Canada are the Ontario lakes especially Lake Simcoe and Lake of Bays; winters in Quebec including old Quebec; fall in the countryside of Nova Scotia and restaurants in Toronto all year long! Of course, the Niagara and Prince Edward County areas for their unbeatable wines too!"

"My children and I made a fun adaptation of this recipe by superb nutritionist Alexia de Macar, whom I had the opportunity to meet at the Cirque du Soleil and then again on the national diving team. It has become a home classic and is a must at family celebrations!"

TRIPLE-FLIP HALF-TWIST DARK CHOCOLATE AND BANANA BREAD

Lysanne Richard
Chicoutimi, QC

World Cup High Diving Champion

SERVINGS 6–8 / PREPARATION 15 MIN / COOKING 1 H

INGREDIENTS

310 ml (1 ¼ cups)	whole wheat flour
5 ml (1 tsp)	baking soda
2 ml (½ tsp)	baking powder
175 ml (¾ cup)	maple syrup
1	egg
1	egg white
60 ml (¼ cup)	low-fat plain yogurt
45 ml (3 tbsp)	vegetable oil
5 ml (1 tsp)	vanilla
3	very ripe medium bananas, mashed
125 ml (½ cup)	dark chocolate chips

PREPARATION

Preheat oven to 180°C (350°F)

1. Butter a 23 x 13–cm (9 x 5–inch) loaf pan. Ensure the pan has capacity for 1.5 L (6 cups).
2. In a bowl, sift together the flour, baking powder and baking soda. Set aside.
3. In another bigger bowl, whisk together the maple syrup, eggs, yogurt, vegetable oil and vanilla. Add bananas and combine.
4. Add dry ingredients and chocolate chips and combine. (Our home special touch is to have the ingredients combined without utensils, by beautiful, and very clean, children's hands.)
5. Pour into the loaf pan. Bake for 1 hour or until a toothpick inserted in the centre of the loaf comes out clean.

" Enjoy with family while telling jokes! "

"Being a Chicoutimi native, I have a special bond with the area and the breathtaking landscapes of the majestic Saguenay Fjord. I'm also very fond of Montreal, my city and its superb emblem, the Olympic Stadium, a wonderful training place where the general public and high performance athletes meet daily."

"This is my mom's recipe that I used to ask for the most when I was growing up. Having Italian heritage, it was a relatively quick recipe for my mom to put together. She would layer hers in one big clear glass bowl but you can put it into individual bowls for a special occasion. The original recipe used both a vanilla and a chocolate pastry cream but due to my severe nut allergy, my mother would only make the vanilla variety."

ZUPPA INGLESE

Alexandre Tagliani
Montreal, QC

Race Car Driver

SERVINGS 12–16 / PREPARATION 30 MIN

INGREDIENTS

Custard

1 L (4 cups)	milk, do not use low-fat or nonfat
2 x 170 ml (⅔ cup)	sugar
10	large egg yolks
125 ml (½ cup)	all-purpose flour
10 ml (2 tsp)	vanilla extract
5 ml (1 tsp)	grated orange peel (optional)

Syrup

280 ml (1 ⅛ cups)	water
180 ml (¾ cup)	sugar
125 ml (½ cup)	cherry liquor

Assembly

1 package	Italian lady finger biscuits
500 ml (2 cups)	chilled whipping cream
	Chocolate shavings (optional)
	Candied fruit, chopped (optional)

PREPARATION

Custard

1. Bring milk and 170 ml (⅔ cup) sugar to a boil in a large heavy saucepan, stirring to dissolve sugar. Remove from heat.
2. Whisk yolks with remaining sugar in a large bowl to blend.
3. Sift flour into yolk mixture and whisk to blend.
4. Gradually whisk in hot milk mixture.
5. Return mixture to the saucepan and whisk over medium heat until the custard boils and thickens, about 2 minutes.
6. Add vanilla and orange peel if desired, and stir to blend.
7. Press plastic wrap onto the surface of custard and chill until cold, at least 4 hours.

Syrup

1. Stir water and sugar in a heavy medium saucepan over medium heat until sugar dissolves.
2. Increase heat and bring to a boil.
3. Let cool.
4. Mix in liquor.

Assembly

1. Arrange lady fingers on bottom of 4 L (16 cups) glass bowl to cover in a single layer.
2. Brush 90 ml (6 tbsp) syrup over.
3. Spread a quarter of custard over cake.
4. Top with another layer of lady fingers.
5. Brush with 105 ml (7 tbsp) syrup.
6. Spread another quarter of custard over.
7. Repeat two more times.
8. Top with a last layer of lady fingers and brush with 105 ml (7 tbsp) syrup.
9. Cover and refrigerate at least 2 hours or overnight.
10. Whip 500 ml (2 cups) chilled cream in a medium bowl to soft peaks and spread over cake.
11. Garnish with chocolate shavings and candied fruit, if desired.
12. Serve.

*"What I like is to take a helicopter tour over Niagara Falls followed by lunch at a local winery.
I also enjoy driving through the mountains in the Laurentians in the fall and taking a stroll through
the streets of Old Montreal as there is so much history and culture to experience."*

INDEX OF PERSONALITIES

INDEX OF RECIPES